hopeful-ISH

I0807737

hopeful-ish

SADNESS, WEARINESS,
DONKEY ATTACKS,
MORE SADNESS,
AND OTHER STUFF
YOU NEED THE
GOSPEL FOR

scarlet hiltibidal

B&H
PUBLISHING®
BRENTWOOD, TENNESSEE

Printed in the United States of America

979-8-3845-1332-2

Published by B&H Publishing Group
Brentwood, Tennessee

Dewey Decimal Classification: 234.2
Subject Heading: HOPE / CHRISTIAN
LIFE / JOY AND SORROW

Cover design by Faceout Studio.
Author photo by Mary Lea Photography.
Images used in the interior were provided by the author.

1 2 3 4 5 • 28 27 26 25

For my mom

Contents

Section 3: Hope Is for Today and Forever

Now may the God of hope fill you with all joy and peace as you believe so that you may overflow with hope by the power of the Holy Spirit. —Romans 15:13

Introduction

I was not ready for the end of the world. I was fourteen, Y2K was looming, my parents were news-on-all-the-time people, and I was nervous. During the actual moment '99 turned to '00, I was standing on the stage in a dark theater for a comedy show. I was not a stand-up comedian. Rather, I was the tag-along daughter of a stand-up comedian. And regardless of the reason I was on that stage that night, the possible apocalypse seemed poised to make the world a sadder, scarier place.

My mom had just finished a set along with Kevin Nealon, Dennis Miller, and Dana Carvey. My little sister and I had been sitting in the wings for the show, when Dennis called us out on stage for the countdown and "Auld Lang Syne." To my pleasant surprise, we got to zero and the world didn't end. Instead, people cheered and kissed and we went back to our fancy water bottles and goodies in the green room. Life surprised us that night by not being sad or tragic.

But that was a long time ago.

Since then, for me and for many, things have often gone the other way. In many ways, the sadness and fear we avoided in 2000 snuck back in twenty years later. Life has been a lot—busy, dangerous, tiresome, even hopeless. Thankfully, that weird Y2K year was the same year I met Jesus, and I have been carrying His hope through every tragedy and heartache I've experienced.

I know I'm not alone in experiencing the exhaustion and sadness of life. And I'm not alone in wanting to hold on to the hope of Christ.

As I write this, it's now been three years since my Uncle Jimmy died by suicide, and my grandma died sixteen days later of Covid-19 pneumonia. And that was just one sixteen-day stretch.

Since that comedy club where the world didn't end, I've been disappointed, despondent, helpless, or heartbroken countless times. As I wrote this book, I learned that my mom's cancer was back. Also as I wrote this book, God decided my family needed one more baby—a surprise, a BOY. The heartaches and shocks and surprises of life haven't slowed down for me even while I try to write a book about hope. Life has kept on life-ing and I need to be reminded of the hope of God more than I even knew.

During the last four years I've said, "I'm sad. I'm tired," over and over again in a loop. Maybe you have too. But even still, even now, there is hope in Jesus, because here's the thing about sadness and exhaustion in the Christian life . . .

> We are hard pressed on every side, but not crushed; perplexed, but not in despair; persecuted, but not abandoned; struck down, but not destroyed. (2 Cor. 4:8–9 NIV)

Sure, sometimes being pressed feels like being crushed. Being perplexed can certainly disguise itself as despair. And being struck down, in the moment, can feel a whole lot like being destroyed. The more believers I've talked to, the less I feel alone in this. Life breaks hearts. There has been so much collective sickness and death and loss and struggles, and even for the Christian, it's hard to remember what's true when you feel like your heart is barely hanging on. But, though my happiness and hyperness have taken a hit, I have real hope I hold onto. I'm writing this to remind me and you that though we are world-weary, though life continues to demand our participation when we just want to hide in a ball in our wearable blankets with our box fans, we are not, in fact, crushed. We are not destroyed. We are not hopeless.

> Though outwardly we are wasting away, yet inwardly we are being renewed day by day. For our light and momentary troubles are achieving for us an eternal glory that far outweighs them all. So we fix our eyes not on what is seen, but on what is unseen, since what is seen is temporary, but what is unseen is eternal. (2 Cor. 4:16b–18 NIV)

The world is always changing and not always for the best. Optimists are wrestling with pessimism. People who were formerly happy and content look at this new world with disappointment and skepticism. Professional lives that used to have excitement and prestige can now be lived on Zoom in Christmas pajama pants. Life just doesn't feel like it used to.

Many relationships have taken a hit and we've lost people we love, and I think we tend to feel pretty beat up. A little sad and tired. Or a lot sad and tired. So, I want this to be a book of hope. I'll share funny stories and heartbreaking ones, many of which have happened in this post-2020 haze, ultimately pointing to the hopeful love story we are living, in light of the gospel. (If you're happy to hear the funny stories but certain types of heartbreaking stories feel especially triggering for you in this season, check out this footnote before moving on.*)

My husband, Brandon, was praying for me and this book the other morning, knowing that hope was not easy to come by for me at that moment, and he said, "God, would you help Scarlet write this book from Your lap? Please let it be beautiful and worshipful and Christ-honoring to the people who will read it."

So, from the Father's lap, I write. I haven't exactly held it together in everything I've been through, but I'm certainly being held. We all are. Those of us who are children of God are in His lap, whether we're celebrating or doubting or feeling stuck in inexpressible pain. He is holding us up and holding us together.

If you've happened to read my first two books (*Afraid of All the Things* and *You're the Worst Person in the World*), you'll remember I wrote about how the gospel has proven strong enough to anchor me—and anchor us all—through the expected storms of anxiety and sin in this life. But, over the past few years, the Lord has been showing me that the gospel is even stronger than I thought. It is also strong enough to hold

* This book includes some details of a family member's suicide. If this is a triggering topic for you, skip to chapter 2.

itself up to deep, dark, unexpected sadnesses. The good news of the gospel of Jesus can get us through anything. Even the worst things.

We believe in a God who has and will overcome even death. We have a God who will restore everything that's been broken. So, I hope that through the pain I share here, you can feel in your hand the thick thread of hope I carry with me, not because I feel strong enough to carry much of anything these days, but because the Spirit of God lives in me and has been carrying me and all my heartaches all along.

If you're a child of God, He can and will do the same for you. So, read on, sad one. If you're too tired, click play on the audiobook version. However you do it, just keep going, because we need each other. We need to share our stories—the ones that looked bleak but turned out redeemed—the ones that seemed sad, but ended up working together for our good (Rom. 8:28). Life is hard. God is holding us. ". . . therefore, we do not lose heart" (2 Cor. 4:16a NIV).

Section 1

Sadness Is Natural—Hope in Sadness Is Supernatural

Blessed be the God and Father of our Lord Jesus Christ. Because of his great mercy he has given us new birth into a living hope through the resurrection of Jesus Christ from the dead.

1 Peter 1:3

Chapter 1

A Broken Rocking Horse and a Broken Heart

Life was good to me on Ventura Boulevard in the '90s. I was harmonizing songs from the Mamas and the Papas with my mom and sister, grabbing black-and-white cookies to and from my mom's auditions, and toting colored pencils in a little pink basket slung over my shoulder. I thought there would only ever be magic on Ventura, until, on a summer day in 2021, I took my husband and daughters to that very same spot for a very different experience. We went to Art's Deli (home of the black-and-white cookie) to have lunch with my most-special, most-funny, most-favorite uncle—Uncle Jimmy.

We looked for parking on the road in the neighborhood right behind the shops. I remembered where the best parking spots were—where we'd pass a coffee shop and my favorite theater-turned-bookstore on the way. It was a happy day and I was the happiest mom, practically wiggling out of my seat and skin with joy as we drove down my hometown roads. We'd just moved across the country for my husband's job in what I viewed to be a grand adventure in Southern California's perfect weather—a move that would also happen to bring me closer to Uncle Jimmy.

He was a father figure, a stand-in dad basically, after my parents divorced and before my mom remarried. He was everything I could have hoped for in a stand-in dad too—he was so funny, completely attentive, knew how to fix my broken rocking horse, and most of all, loved me. I had no doubt in my mind that he loved me.

When we got to Art's Deli that 2021 summer day, the black-and-white cookies were there. I even recognized one of the managers behind the counter. There was plenty of nostalgia that lived up to my expectations, but not Uncle Jimmy. Uncle Jimmy wasn't doing well.

The first words out of his mouth weren't good ones. One of the stronger of the four-letter variety spilled out before I had the chance to cover my little ones' ears. He talked about himself and the world with a heartbreaking amount of cynicism and pessimism. Though he was acting strange, and though the degree to which he wasn't taking care of himself was noticeable, I tried to make conversation and act normal while I worried about whether or not he was okay. Nothing about him looked right. He was really red and disheveled and fidgety the whole time. The levity and nostalgia and love I'd hoped for in that lunch was hijacked by what felt like a deep darkness coming from someone I loved so much. I got through our lunch, and fought through the sadness of seeing someone I loved so much doing so poorly. As we got back in the car, my attention shifted to trying to figure out how to debrief on the ride home with the girls. *How was I to explain the things they'd just heard and witnessed?*

It hadn't been that long since I'd seen Jimmy. Just six months earlier, he'd flown to see us in Tennessee and spent Christmas in a cabin with us, with my parents, and his mom, my beloved Grandma Marlene. You can read more about that fiasco in my last book, *You're the Worst Person in the World*, but in short, it wasn't the smoothest Christmas gathering.

Something I didn't share when I wrote about that Christmas was how Uncle Jimmy was doing. He was really down and really drinking. And making a lot of comments (he called them jokes) about suicide.

He'd recently lost his job due to Covid cutbacks and gone through a break-up with his fiancé. He'd just been engaged for the first time, at sixty years old, and it didn't work out. It was hard to be in the same room with him that Christmas. Sometimes, we'd be eating a meal together, and he would just have tears streaming down his face. He'd been sad and tired for a long time.

I knew that. We all knew that. And we all tried to help and encourage him, but I was busy being a busy mom with a busy life. I was busy being happy, honestly, and sometimes it's hard to look at hopelessness and know what to say or how to help.

I did try. We all did. He was my special person, after all. Do you have someone like that? We'd always had a bond. A few years prior to our move, he told me that the PIN number he'd used for everything in his life was my birthday and that it always had been, because "I knew I could never have any negative association with that number."

I wanted to help him in his suffering, but I stumbled over my words, trying to share my own story of moving from hopelessness to hopefulness and joy. I stumbled, because it can be awkward to try to help someone who helped raise you. Like, *Who am I to say something to him? He changed my diapers.*

Just a month after moving into our new California house, when the Ikea bed frames I ordered for my girls came in, my husband was busy starting his new job, and I had the passing thought, *I should call Uncle Jimmy and ask him to put these beds together.* But I didn't call. I didn't want to bother him. I had just spoken to him on the phone after his neighbor called my parents, worried about his well-being. My parents were out of the country, so my dad called my husband, Brandon, and asked us to check on him. The check-in didn't go great, and under the circumstances, asking him to put beds together didn't seem like the thing to do, so I brushed the thought aside and continued my happy, coffee-fueled morning of furniture assembling and settling into our new home in our new city, thousands of miles away from all family and friends. But at least Uncle Jimmy was there. He was near, and he'd get better. I just knew it. I put three beds together in two days and I was so proud of myself.

Then, just a handful of weeks after I'd put those beds together, I was cleaning out the litter box for my daughters' pet rabbits, and I got a phone call. If I had to pick the moment that I went from being hopeful and hyper to sad and tired, that was probably the moment.

I was hunched over the rabbits with the Lysol wipes and the garbage bag when the phone started ringing. I answered it. It was my mom.

"Scarlet, I have to tell you something bad," she said.

And the next few moments just felt impossible.

"Jimmy killed himself this morning," she said. ". . . Are you still there?"

I couldn't respond for a moment. Honestly, as I write this, it still feels impossible to me. Sometimes, I can't believe it's true.

I remember hearing a preacher once who said the reason death doesn't compute, doesn't sit right with us, is because we are eternal beings. We were created to live forever in perfect peace with God. Death doesn't sit right with us because it's so unnatural. We were created to live forever.

But this felt like more than death, worse than death, bigger than death. I know sin broke the world and brought death along with it. But suicide? My Uncle Jimmy? It just felt too wrong, too horrible, too hopeless. My head started throbbing. I had no words.

That horrible day, August 7, 2021, I felt nearly crushed by hopelessness.

Jimmy was part of me. Part of the fabric that made me who I am. His presence and laughter and humor are intertwined into so many of my formative memories. There are little things I do that I learned from him. When I make spaghetti, I sing, "Gone fishin', in a shady wady pool . . ." and stick a solitary spaghetti noodle in like it's a fishing rod until it goes limp.

I knew Jimmy. I knew his kindness, his creativity. And I could see that the lies he believed that led to him ending his life were just that—lies. But as grief and guilt and sadness and confusion pressed me from all angles that horrible day, which dragged into months, which spilled into years, hopeless thinking started seeping into my mind too. Cynicism, doubt, despair, hopelessness, or as our good friend, Jake, says, "the deep sad." The former hyper-happy version of me felt like a slap in the face to a world where the unthinkable can just happen right in the middle of cleaning a rabbit's litter box. A world where you think the garbage bag of bunny droppings is going to be the worst part of your day, only to receive a phone call that crushes you with the horror of the worst realities that exist in this so fallen, so broken world. That hyper-happy me was gone.

The deep sad set in.

Dewy Floats

My husband gets nervous when our kids are in the water, because, his words, "Humans are land creatures." Even now that they can swim, it makes him uncomfortable.

A few years ago, we were at a friend's house and our kids were swimming in their pool and Dewy said to Brandon, "Daddy, can I go to the deep end?"

"I don't know, love, I'm not sure you're ready for that yet."

A few minutes later, she said, "Daddy, can I get in the hot tub?"

"I don't know, love, that water gets pretty choppy."

Then, "Daddy, watch me do a trick."

"Please be careful, love, you don't really know how to swim yet."

Finally, our friend said to him, "Bro, calm down, she's wearing a life vest."

And she was. She never got in a pool, at that point, without a life vest. So, in spite of any parental anxiety or worry, Dewy couldn't sink.

It doesn't matter how deep the water is. Dewy can't sink. It doesn't matter how choppy it gets. Dewy can't sink. It doesn't matter if she can't quite execute her water twirl or even if a sister smashes into her in the water. Dewy has a life vest, so Dewy can't sink. Dewy floats.

That is what the gospel offers our hearts, even in the midst of the deep sad.

In the book of 1 Peter, the apostle Peter is writing to Christians in the first century and to Christians today, helping us realize that in all the seeming hopelessness we live in, we have, in Jesus, something that cannot sink. We have living hope. Unsinkable hope.

Do you have a real hope that functions for you like Dewy's life vest? Do you have something that keeps your soul buoyed in dark days? Do you have anything in your life that supports your joy when your joy finds itself descending into the depths?

You don't need me to convince you that you will have those seasons. We know the world we live in is a world of suffering. In fact, my daughter Dewy's real name is Brooklyn Hope Hiltibidal. Brooklyn means "from the land of the broken" and we wanted our daughter's name to mean "hope in the land of the broken." But then, our oldest started calling her "Dewy." Doesn't quite have the same spiritual impact.

My Dewy aside, we live in the land of the broken and we know it. We live in a world of sickness and suicide. Ours is a land of political turmoil, economic doubt, and actual wars. We live in the home of the deep sad.

And you have whatever brokenness is in your mind right now that you are currently living with. Maybe your chin today is just above the water line of hopelessness. What hope do we have?

Well, Peter, writing 2,000 years ago, under the direction of the Holy Spirit, was writing to us, yes, but his original audience was a people in a more difficult situation than anything we find ourselves in.

Look at the first two verses of 1 Peter, chapter 1:

> Peter, an apostle of Jesus Christ: To those chosen, living as exiles dispersed abroad in Pontus, Galatia, Cappadocia, Asia, and Bithynia, chosen according to the foreknowledge of God the Father, through the sanctifying work of the Spirit, to be obedient and to be sprinkled with the blood of Jesus Christ. May grace and peace be multiplied to you.

The first hearers of Peter's letter were "those chosen, living as exiles dispersed abroad." This is super important for our understanding of hope. Peter was writing to Christians in unfathomably difficult circumstances. Strong hostility and opposition forced them out of town, and so they became exiles, dispersed around the nations. Peter was writing at the beginning of one of the most intense seasons of persecution in the history of the church. Christians were being exiled and marginalized, and very soon, Christians would be killed.

And it's not like they didn't have all the other struggles we have. They had our difficulties worse than we have them. The Christians in the first century had Mondays, but they didn't have Keurigs. They broke bones, but there was no Ibuprofen. I've read that the average lifespan at this time in history was thirty-five to forty years old.[1] We can't even really imagine their lives.

Short, difficult lives in the face of harsh persecution, and Peter says to them,

> . . . chosen according to the foreknowledge of God the Father, through the sanctifying work of the Spirit, to be obedient and to be sprinkled with the blood of Jesus Christ. May grace and peace be multiplied to you. (v. 2)

But it's in the next three verses that the living hope shows up.

> Blessed be the God and Father of our Lord Jesus Christ. Because of his great mercy he has given us new birth into a living hope through the resurrection of Jesus Christ from the dead and into an inheritance that is imperishable, undefiled, and unfading, kept in heaven for you. You are being guarded by God's power

> through faith for a salvation that is ready to be revealed in the last time. (vv. 3–5)

How beautiful. Peter writes, "[God] . . . has *given* us new birth into a living hope through the resurrection of Jesus Christ from the dead."

What I pray our hearts can hold onto as we look for hope in this life is that hope is a gift. It is a gift, because it is an outcome of the new birth that is only available through the resurrection of Jesus. Again, He "has given us new birth into a living hope."

There was certainly nothing I could do to give myself hope, lying on the floor when I had that phone call with my mom. I couldn't find hope; I had to be filled with it. We can't grab hope; we have to be given it. And when it is given to us through Jesus, Peter tells us what it looks like.

Jesus's hope is, of many things, the hope of a perfect future. "Because of his great mercy he has given us new birth into a living hope through the resurrection of Jesus Christ from the dead and *into an inheritance that is imperishable, undefiled, and unfading, kept in heaven for you*" (vv. 3–4, emphasis added).

Most people rush to the second half of that passage. We have hope, many think, because one day we'll make it to the golden shores of heaven where we'll inherit all that is imperishable, undefiled, and unfading. We can keep hanging on because one day, many say, we'll go from the chaos, tears, death, grief, and pain of right now to the peace of Revelation 21:4: "Death will be no more; grief, crying, and pain will be no more, because the previous things have passed away."

And the many are right. All of that is true. In Jesus, we do have the sure hope of a heavenly future and eternal inheritance. This perfect future is something we are given by God. But that's not all Peter says we are given. He says we're also given a present hope. Look again at the passage, but this time, focus on the tense of when our hope was given:

> Because of his great mercy he *has* given us new birth into a living hope through the resurrection of Jesus Christ from the dead and into an inheritance that is imperishable, undefiled, and unfading, kept in heaven for you. (vv. 3–4, emphasis added)

Do we have to wait to enter into the living hope God promises us? No. God has already given this to us. It's for today, not just tomorrow.

In other words, heaven may be a deferred experience for us, but hope isn't. This means our perspective can shift from "I'm going to suffer in this world, but one day it will all be worth it in heaven" to "Yes, one day it will all be worth it, but it is also worth it right now." Because Peter said we have a living hope right now. What God wants to give us—no, has *already given us*—is not just a far-away future hope, it is a living, right-now hope.

What that means is that hope in Jesus is the only hope you can have right now that you can keep. Jesus is a living hope as opposed to everything else being a dying hope.

Maybe you started a new relationship recently. You've found the guy or girl you hope is the one. You've got butterflies. You hope that person makes you happy for the rest of your life. But think about those last five words . . . "the rest of your life." The relationship that gives you butterflies, no matter what, is doomed. Even if it lasts every day of your life, your life will end one day, and the relationship with it. Any human relationship is, by default, a dying hope.

Maybe you hope that you are going to get a new dream job this year. I hope that for you too, but it is a dying hope. The moment you have that job, you are moving, inescapably, toward not having that job. The same goes for houses or dogs or kids.

Don't worry, this book will get happier.

It's true, though. Every single thing we pursue in this world is a thing that we can't keep. This is the case with every possible hope outside of the soul-shaping, life-vested love of the God of the universe. Every hope apart from Jesus is a hope with an end date. Earthly hopes have shelf lives. There comes a point where even if the hope is fulfilled, there is nothing left to hope for. The best marriages end. The best jobs end. The best hobbies end. So do the best uncles. There's only one hope that isn't a dying hope.

> Jesus Christ is the same yesterday, today, and forever. (Heb. 13:8)

Jesus is a living, eternal friend. Jesus has a living, eternal love. Because He cannot die, everything that radiates from Him toward us cannot die either, whether that's His love or mercy or friendship or *hope*. Said another way, you have a living hope in Jesus because *Jesus Himself* is living—He overcame death in His resurrection, and He'll never die again. He's alive. Forever, unchangeably alive. This means the hope He gives you is alive too, and cannot give out, run out of steam, or die on you.

Only the mercy of the living Jesus can heal us. Only the presence of the living God can satisfy us. And He can do that, regardless of our brokenness. We live in hope-adverse times; we are hopeful-ish at best, but Jesus isn't thrown off course by what happens on this earth. And He's never going anywhere. That makes His hope a present hope. It's a living hope. It is something supernatural that you have been given in Jesus, and because you have been given it, it is something you can do. Because you have hope, you can hope.

The Greek word for hope, in 1 Peter 1:3 is *elpis*, and *elpis* means "the expectation of good." *Elpis* is what I had in the '90s on Ventura Blvd. But it is so easy to lose hold of in this life. The Christian life, though, can mean the expectation of good. The hope we have in the gospel is a hope that expects good. Because when we're in Jesus, the Living Hope, the one who always guards, and gives mercy, and leads, and loves, even our seasons of pain come with the expectation of future good.

> You rejoice in this, even though now for a short time, if necessary, you suffer grief in various trials so that the proven character of your faith—more valuable than gold which, though perishable, is refined by fire—may result in praise, glory, and honor at the revelation of Jesus Christ. Though you have not

> seen him, you love him; though not seeing him now, you believe in him, and you rejoice with inexpressible and glorious joy, because you are receiving the goal of your faith, the salvation of your souls. (1 Pet. 1:6–9)

Peter is saying that Jesus is so good, so glorious, and so for us that in the face of suffering, our expectation for good can be so strong that we rejoice. Jesus gives us hope, and when we experience that hope, we can act on it in any circumstance.

God Supernaturally Comforts

I think the older we get, the harder it is to hold on to hope when the world breaks our hearts. The more disappointments we rack up, the harder and more protective our hearts get. Lord, help us stay soft. Yes, death exists. Yes, life isn't fair in the worst ways. But, I think that the miracle of walking with Jesus, walking with the Spirit of God, is His ability to re-soften us, to restore us, to reclaim what our enemy meant for evil.

> We know that all things work together for the good of those who love God, who are called according to his purpose. (Rom. 8:28)

Sadness is natural. Sadness is to be expected. Sadness is inevitable. But experiencing hope in the midst of sadness is supernatural. Jesus can help us experience soul-level hope, even while our hearts are sad. We can have hope that souls are eternal, that life is restorable, and that broken things are fixable, through the power of God.

Uncle Jimmy was able to fix my broken rocking horse, but he wasn't able to fix himself. Jesus is able to fix broken hearts and fix them forever. The hope He gives to the hopeless is a gift. He has compassion on those who suffer and doubt and struggle. We can bring Him our losses and our questions and our pains—our deep sad—and He knows what to do with them. Because He's alive, He knows how to give us lasting and living hope right now, exactly when we need it. His hope is for today. Lysol, garbage bags, and all.

Uncle Jimmy, broken rocking horse, and me, 1989.

Chapter 2

Fake Farming . . . Weary Worship: I Want the Real Thing

I used to be a fake farmer. Between the years of 2017 and 2021, we had a few acres and a few chickens and a few failed gardens. Growing up a city girl, my first go-around with country life was an adjustment. I loved what it looked like out the window, from inside. I loved watching my girls collect eggs and throw rocks in the creek. But I didn't like the poisonous copperhead we found in said creek, or the task of pulling ticks out of our persons and animals with tweezers. I didn't like having to drive twenty-plus minutes to fill up my gas tank or take Joy to school. I didn't like all the baby chicken funerals, the duck funerals—*so many funerals*—or the threats from nearby country neighbors when our dog tried to eat their chickens. There was a lot about country life I was happy to say goodbye to. The whole time I was there, I was half in. I lived there because I lived there, but I didn't garden or walk beside the creek or take advantage of all the beauty around me.

Then, in 2021, we made our big move out to sunny, ocean-breezy Orange County, California. I rarely saw a bug. I never witnessed an animal death, not one, in the time we lived there. And I loved it. It was familiar. It was easy. It was clean. But I learned early on that the magic of California weather couldn't stop the heartaches we would walk through out there.

The day Uncle Jimmy died, I drove to the last place I saw him. It was a restaurant in Huntington Beach called Lemonade. Jimmy had never been, so he let me order for him. We both got the same thing—the mango chicken bowl—a spicy bowl of red rice, purple kale, honey roasted Brussels, and Thai sauce with lavender lemonade to drink. Very California. I'd taken Jimmy to Lemonade just a couple of weeks before he died, and the day I got the news, I didn't know what to do with my grief. So, I repeated the last day I'd had with him, except this time I did it alone. I drove to Pacific City, parked in the parking garage, and went up the escalator we'd taken together. Then, I went to the counter at Lemonade and ordered the mango chicken bowl and the lavender lemonade. I sat at the same table and picked at my food. I sat in the seat he'd been in just weeks earlier when we took photos with my girls, a smiling photo and a "silly" one. I never know what to do when someone says to pose for a silly photo. Neither did he. He just smiled in both.

I don't know what comfort I thought I'd find in recreating our last day together, but it didn't work. The next thing I did was drive to Target. I remember buying sweatpants, a sweatshirt, and dark sunglasses. That didn't help either.

The months that followed were a blur of sadness. Of looking for comfort, having nightmares, getting stuck on *the questions* that plague the loved ones of those who die by suicide.

It's one thing to have faith in your faith when living is easy, but moments like those? Everything turns into a question. A life-or-death, heaven-or-hell question.

The California weather had no answers for such questions and the pain made us think of home.

I remember my youngest, Dewy, my farmiest of farm girls sighing one day as she sidewalk-chalked the pavers behind our house: "I miss grass." California was in no way void of nature. The ocean and sand and sky-high palms were a different kind of beauty and we lived a different kind of life. But two years into our West Coast adventure, we decided to move back home to the grassy, snakey, green hills of Tennessee, and our Zillow searches had a filter that said, "5 acres or more."

We couldn't wait to get back. And when we did, we decided to stop being "pretend farmers" and do it up real. I even intentionally switched some of my lingo to include phrases like "do it up real." I went from "you guys" to "y'all." We would not take our country-ness for granted this time. Not if I had anything to do with it.

Goodbye Lunches and Green Pastures

One of the big reasons we moved back to Tennessee was because that's where my family is and where Brandon's family planned to move. His family had lived in the Carolinas, but because of job transitions and our family's decision to move back closer, they decided to join us in the Volunteer State. It was something we had talked about for years that was finally happening.

Brandon's parents bought a house five minutes down the road from us. My mother-in-law teaches voice and piano, and she gave the girls free lessons every week. Brandon's sister, her husband, and their two kids moved too, before they even sold their South Carolina house.

They lived with Brandon's parents for a few months, but ultimately ended up returning to South Carolina when their house wouldn't sell. Then, just five months later, Brandon's parents ended up moving back to South Carolina, too. Within less than a year, Brandon's whole family came and went.

On top of that, the pastor at the church we'd been part of in Tennessee moved away, and four of the closest friends Brandon was excited to get back in his life had separate lunches with him where they shared that they were also moving away, for various reasons.

It felt like a practical joke. Literally, every single thing and/or person that motivated Brandon's return to Tennessee was gone within a year. He and I couldn't help but wrestle with more *whys*.

Me and my girls, on the other hand, transitioned right back into the life we'd left. California ended up feeling like an extended vacation, as our friends and our homeschool-hybrid group and my family were right where we'd left them.

We tried to fall back into our Tennessee rhythms, despite the unexpected changes. We moved into the farmhouse and bought a new flock of chickens. A new mower. New cowboy boots and overalls. A page was turned. A new level was attained. Two donkeys arrived and legitimized our farming dreams.

Sure, not everything had worked out just right, but we had a roof over our heads, people we loved nearby, and so much of that green grass that we'd missed as Californians.

The arrival of the donkeys felt like a very big moment. Like, an official farm moment. We named them Buddy and Jake. Buddy was a mini who instantly adored us. Jake, full-sized and slow to befriend, needed to be bribed. And really, it wasn't just the getting of the donkeys that turned me into a real farmer. No. It was the incident with the gate.

A few days into having donkeys, as they continued to warm up to us, we realized they were hovering as far away from their water source and shelter as donk-ily possible. The gate we needed—the one that would keep them in the right spot—hadn't arrived yet, so I did what any true and seasoned farmer would do—I made a temporary gate by way of red rope, extension cords, and moving blankets.

I was so proud of myself. It was homemade. It was effective. It was the solution to our gate-waiting donkey-watering. Until it was not.

A day before our new gate came, Buddy, the mini, the sweetheart, escaped under the extension cord. *No biggie,* I thought, *I will just bring him back. I am a farmer! I am MacGyver. I am Old McDonald.*

So I walked out into the field he'd escaped to, and as I approached our sweet little mini, he started charging at me, wide-eyed, practically foaming at the mouth and saying, in plain English, "HEE HA HEE HAW HEE HAW HEE HAW." Yes, like a cartoon.

I fled toward the gate and told my youngest daughter, who was with me to "RUN!"

We jumped over the "gate" I was so proud of to safety—gasping and recovering from what seemed to be a near miniature-donkey-double-homicide.

It is funny to reflect on, but in the moment, it was genuinely terrifying.

Though I thought the "real farmer" in me kicked in when I crafted a donkey barrier with household objects, I think it actually kicked in the day after the Buddy incident, when my daughters and I helped my husband install a real gate and reestablished friendship with Buddy and Jake.

From Flimsy Peace to the Real Thing

I wouldn't say I was ever a "pretend Christian" the way I was a "pretend farmer," but I was certainly, for a long stretch in my teen years and early adulthood, calling myself a Christian while ultimately living for myself rather than for God.

Jesus said, "I have come so that they may have life and have it in abundance" (John 10:10b), but abundant life always seemed to elude me. My life wasn't abundant because my life wasn't reflecting the real thing.

When I was fourteen, I made a commitment to Jesus. I prayed a prayer and got baptized and quickly went from embracing real peace in Jesus to trying to find it in my performance for Jesus.

In my teens, I developed what I thought was a fool-proof peace formula that involved making everyone in my school and family and life worship me for my awesomeness, with some Jesus sprinkled on top.

My twenties? So glad you asked. Peace, at that age, looked like protection—I worked to protect myself from pain, from embarrassment, from anything that could threaten my comfort. Again, I was a Christian, but living like a fake farmer . . . wearing the overalls and the muck boots, with little to no harvest.

And now, here in the later part of my thirties, I find myself behaving so frequently like the Israelites throughout the Old Testament. They had experienced the real thing so many times—the fire and smoke of God leading them through the wilderness, the food falling from heaven when they needed it most, the water provided for them when they were thirsty, and so on. And yet, as if on cue, they cycled through the same forgetfulness, fretting, and frustration toward God on the other side of all those miracles. They even started faking it with God, keeping with the external rules for life He had laid out, but with reluctance and grumbling and an eye toward false gods.

I, too, have experienced the real thing in Jesus—the real peace, the real joy, the real moments of provision when there's no other explanation but God. And yet on the other side of it, when life goes from the miracle to the mundane and starts to feel like an unruly miniature donkey, I start forgetting and fretting and losing sight of hope. And like the Israelites, I start faking it.

Don't Fake Your Faith

I was out of town earlier this year, speaking at a women's event, and during the discussion time, after one of my talks, I sat down and listened to women of all walks of life talk through their varying faith journeys. Some of the women were clearly new believers. I remember one of them telling me she hadn't read the Bible and had barely attended church, and she wanted me to tell her how to follow Jesus. I remember feeling that her question was too big for me to answer. There's an entire "living and active" book about that, after all. How could I possibly put into just a few sentences what it means to have a real relationship with the Rescuer of the world? Thankfully, I don't have to.

Jesus already summarized the whole thing for us, when He came to earth.

> When the Pharisees heard that he had silenced the Sadducees, they came together. And one of them, an expert in the law, asked a question to test him: "Teacher, which command in the law is the greatest?" He said to him, "Love the Lord your God with all your heart, with all your soul, and with all your mind. This is the greatest and most important command. The second is like it: Love your neighbor as yourself. All the Law and the Prophets depend on these two commands." (Matt. 22:34–40)

That's the real thing. That's the answer.

I opened my laptop today to work on this chapter—this chapter I outlined a year ago. A year ago, I planned to write this chapter about real farming versus fake farming, real faith versus phony faith. And today, before I opened God's Word, I asked Him to help me do it. I said out loud, "Lord, help me write an encouraging book right now." I asked the Lord that because I was very focused on the fact that our upstairs AC unit is out and that we may have just paid some guy $600 to try and fail at fixing it. Another stressor. Another let-down. The me of today wondered how I'd conjure up a "hopeful-ish" message without a fully functioning air conditioner.

And then I looked at God's Word. I looked at the commands of Jesus to love, remembering how He loved. The AC is still broken but I got to remember how He loves.

It's hard to stay cynical when you remember how loved you are, how much you've been forgiven, how the "unfairness" of life has really worked in your favor.

None of us deserve a cush life with an always-working air conditioner and a perfectly fulfilling career and relational life that never lets us down. We deserve nothing, but in Christ, we have everything.

Because of Jesus, room temperature problems and health problems and hope problems will one day cease. If we're living for forever instead of for right now, we can be soft-hearted. We can be joyful. We can be instruments of love and encouragement in the lives of those around us.

Even at seven months pregnant with a broken HVAC in the dead of summer.

The Gift of a Broken HVAC

This is the second summer we've lived in our house and the second summer we've had an HVAC unit decide to die in ninety-degree temperatures. Last year, it was the unit that cools the main part of our house. Impossible. Miserable. Sweltering. So we got it replaced. A man saved in my phone as "Keith AC guy" swooped in and solved our problems in exchange for many dollars.

This year, it was our second, smaller unit that went out, so the only rooms affected were the bedrooms of our two youngest daughters, who basically live for special nights on the foldout couch bed downstairs—a treat that usually only happens when I'm out of town traveling for work.

"Girls, you all are going to have to spend some nights on the couch bed while we get the AC unit worked out."

The joy was instant, palpable, and voluminous. So much rejoicing. So much celebration. While Dad and I were wringing our hands over the big expenses that come with home ownership, the littles were rejoicing in their forced slumber party, their change of bedtime scenery, and their close proximity to our bedroom.

My youngest told me that she loves sleeping downstairs because she loves being on the same floor as Mommy and Daddy.

It struck me, how beautiful it is, that the obvious discomfort and inconvenience of sauna-like summer bedrooms was overshadowed by the happiness of two little girls who get to sleep together and be closer to Mom and Dad.

If only I viewed hardship that way. If only I saw suffering, big and small, the way the Bible paints it: as an ever-present opportunity for more dependence on and closeness with my heavenly Father. As a way to draw closer to my spiritual siblings as we wait out the night together. The stunning nature of the Christian life is that this viewpoint is true. The seasons of hurting are always a chance to celebrate moving closer to Dad.

The Gift of Pain and Real Happiness

C. S. Lewis wrote a book called *The Problem of Pain*, and in it he talked about how difficult it is to be happy in Jesus when the surface-y things of life are going well for us. He wrote,

> If the first and lowest operation of pain shatters the illusion that all is well, the second shatters the illusion that what we have, whether good or bad in itself, is our own and enough for us. Everyone has noticed how hard it is to turn our thoughts to God when everything is going well with us. We "have all we want" is a terrible saying when "all" does not include God. We find God an interruption. As St. Augustine says somewhere, "God wants to give us something, but cannot, because our hands are full—there's nowhere for Him to put it." Or as a friend of mine said, "We regard God as an airman regards his parachute; it's

> there for emergencies but he hopes he'll never have to use it." Now God, who has made us, knows what we are and that our happiness lies in Him. Yet we will not seek it in Him as long as He leaves us any other resort where it can even plausibly be looked for. While what we call "our own life" remains agreeable we will not surrender it to Him. What then can God do in our interests but make "our own life" less agreeable to us, and take away the plausible source of false happiness?[2]

Oof. If that doesn't make you feel something, your hands might be overwhelmingly full. I know mine often are. I'm aware that a broken HVAC unit only affecting two rooms is a very "first-world problem," as they say. But, lately, this year in particular, my family has faced several heavier disappointments, and I've struggled to remain hopeful as painful circumstances have piled up.

I forget what a gift we have in the simple presence of God. I forget that going to Him is what I was made for; His presence, in the end, is all there is. I forget that every temporary thing I long to have here on earth is a gift meant to point me to His creativity, help me depend on His care, and lead me to bask in His glory. As Lewis said, "God wants to give us something," and it's THAT something which will give us real happiness, not the kind of flimsy happiness we can find from a controlled home temperature or a fun phone game or a compliment from our spouse or a bonus at work.

I want real happiness. I want the lasting kind and I want it for my family too. Happiness that can't be taken away when lesser comforts are removed.

I want the Psalm 1 kind of happiness.

> How happy is the one who does not walk in the advice of the wicked or stand in the pathway with sinners or sit in the company of mockers! Instead, his delight is in the LORD's instruction, and he meditates on it day and night. He is like a tree planted beside flowing streams that bears its fruit in its season, and its leaf does not wither. Whatever he does prospers. The wicked are not like this; instead, they are like chaff that the wind blows away. Therefore the wicked will not stand up in the judgment, nor sinners in the assembly of the righteous. For the LORD watches over the way of the righteous, but the way of the wicked leads to ruin.

I want it so much, and I know where to find it. It's a gift when the HVAC goes out, or when the loved ones move away, or when the job doesn't pan out. It's a gift because we can much more easily see our need for God, and we can much more appreciate the kind of closeness that He offers. It's in the drought we most notice the flowing streams. God wants to be with us and actually make us happy in Him.

Charles Spurgeon said that the original word for "happy" in this verse is plural and that therefore it is pointing to the multiple incredible blessings that we have in the Lord. He said we really should think of this word as "felicity" or "bliss" and that we should read it as "Oh the blessedesses!"[3]

That sounds awesome, right? But sometimes life gets shaky. When the wind comes, the non-blessed person is blown away. Without roots and without water, the plant withers in adversity and is thrown about like chaff. But that is not the case for the happy soul.

Of course, the happy soul isn't happy because everything is perfect. It is happy because of where it is planted.

I love it when the Bible is its own illustration—what this is saying is that your soul is like a tree that *will* know dry days and stormy weather. In this life, there will be seasons of doubt or confusion or fear just like the tree will know dark days of drought or wind or frost. The picture in Psalm 1 is not a tree that never knows lack. No. But it is a tree that will still bear fruit in its season. It is a tree that will not wither when difficulty comes. And that is because in all seasons and all circumstances the tree is planted where its roots always receive life from the river.

You can lose your job but not lose your hope when you are rooted in God, the inexhaustible river of hope. You can have cancer, but if you are planted in God, you still have life and even life forever. You can endure any season when your roots go down deep to a River that has never failed and never will fail.

Happy souls are planted by rivers of water. Happy souls are happy, not because we have willed life into our leaves. We are happy because of the strength of the river.

"The Lord watches over the way of the righteous." In Hebrew, that phrase "watches over" means "known."[4] One commentator I read said this word shows an "intimate acquaintance with God as an expression of His love and care."[5] In other words, the happy soul is seen and known. If you are a Christian, this is the ultimate hope for your soul.

Is there any happier, more hopeful thought than that of being watched over by God? It is relational. It is secure. The wicked perish. The righteous are watched over. The righteous are known by God.

There are rabbits all over our farm. We see rabbits every day. It's not an exaggeration to say you can hardly go outside at our house without seeing a rabbit. But I don't know those rabbits. My family doesn't have a relationship with them. We don't protect them. None of the rabbits on our farm enjoy our special care—except two.

Puffy and Floppsie are our rabbits. We don't just see them. We know them. We love them. We feed them. We have concern for them. We protect them. The rabbits that live in the woods around my house will live two to three years on average. They are going to perish. But not the bunnies we know. Not the ones we watch over. Not Puffy and Flopsie. They've already lived longer than that. They have protection. They have food every day. They get prayed for in family prayer. My daughter, Ever, wants Puffy to live the longest life of any bunny ever, and Puffy has a shot at it because she is known and loved and watched over by someone who, even with limited power, can care for her.

And in the eyes of God, you and I are Puffy and Flopsie. His children are seen and known and loved by the God of limitless power. How happy to be watched over by the God of the universe. How happy to be planted by the river in all seasons.

We can be like little kids on a couch bed, hearing the sounds of our parents just a few feet away . . . secure in their protection, secure in their love. I want that. Don't you?

Here's the good news: we can have that. All we need is Jesus.

So, What's the Real Thing?

Real, true Jesus-following is daily leading yourself to depend on the Lord, to acknowledge the Creator and Savior, to thank Him and ask Him and bless Him and cry to Him. To run to His Word for life, guidance, comfort, and help. To turn your eyes from false, flimsy, or short-lived sources of hope and run to the true and living Source. To live and breathe prayers, so you can see how very ever present He is, how generous He is, how involved He is, how real He is. Not because good Christians do this stuff or because you need to go through the motions to keep up good appearances but because you need these things to live. The fruits of the Christian life are only phony when we look for them in the wrong places.

God is only always real and good. Sometimes, in my weakness, I struggle to believe that's true.

I was a real farmer the week we had donkeys delivered. But all I have to do to stop living the farm life is . . . stop living the farm life. All I have to do is stay in my *most-of-the-time* air-conditioned house or give away some animals and get some new hobbies and I'll forget. I'll forget being hee-hawed at. I'll forget the feeling of raising chickens. I could even forget fresh air and open space and that would be alright.

But I don't want to ever forget the Lord. He's the REAL real thing. His joy unspeakable and full of glory is the one thing we really can't live without.

Christians don't move on from experiencing God, so I don't want to fake it for my family, fake it for my friends, fake it for my readers. I want the real thing today, with Jesus. And I want to hear from Him again tomorrow. I'm praying the same for you, farmers and non-farmers alike.

I hope that if you woke up sad and hopeless feeling today, you are able to remember and repent and return and rejoice. That is so the Christian life. Remember . . . repent . . . return . . . rejoice. Remember . . . repent . . . return . . . rejoice.

I currently live on a farm and there are a bunch of animals outside that will die if I don't give them food and water. I don't always feel "farm-y," but that doesn't mean I stop taking care of them. In fact, I don't feel very farmy right now. But, when I walked outside to look at some model number thing on our broken AC Unit, Jake the donkey hee-hawed at me because he was ready to be let out of the stable. What if I said, "Sorry, Jake, I don't feel like being farmy. No grass for you today"?

For Jake, for me to stop farming "because I don't feel farmy" is absurd. If I want to be farmy, all I really need to do is just keep living the farm life. Keep letting Jake out. Keep feeding the chickens. Keep filling the water troughs. And not because I need to sustain some charade in front of others. But because *this little farm world needs these rhythms to live.*

In the same way, we don't take our eyes off of Jesus because life isn't what we want it to be or because we don't feel "Christiany" today. I mean, we can. And sometimes, we do. But how miserable is the Christian who isn't walking with Jesus . . . who isn't living the Christ life?

> "Abide in me, and I in you. As the branch cannot bear fruit by itself, unless it abides in the vine, neither can you, unless you abide in me. I am the vine; you are the branches. Whoever abides in me and I in him, he it is that bears much fruit, for apart from me you can do nothing." (John 15:4–5 ESV)

Abiding is returning to His Word, His presence, His church, His people, even when we don't feel like it. *Especially* when we don't feel like it. Even when the sadness feels crushing, we can still abide. We can keep showing up to the water, especially when our roots and our hearts are dry. We can keep receiving the nourishment of the Word, particularly when our weariness finds its craving for stability and strength at an all-time high. Not because we need to keep up appearances, but because we need—now more than ever—these rhythms to live. *Because we need God.* That's not phoniness. That's just self-control and wisdom. That's not going through the motions. That's running to the *right* place for comfort and sustainment when you're about to collapse. That's not fake; that's the Christ life.

But maybe you have kids or coworkers or fellow small groupers at church that you feel like you need to put on a hope-filled face for. To that, I'd say, let's ask the Lord to turn our phoniness into faith. Let's keep trusting Him to turn our wandering to worshipping. Let's be real. And seek. And find. And fix our eyes on Jesus, the "founder and perfecter of our faith, who for the joy that was set before him endured the cross, despising the shame, and is seated at the right hand of the throne of God" (Heb. 12:2 ESV).

I don't know if you're sitting down to work on a Christian book today or hunching over to chase a toddler or clocking in at a job that you kind of hate. Whatever it is, God is with you today and you can come to Him with your faith-tank full or with a heart that feels empty and let-down. He knows how to comfort. He is the River. *He knows you.* He is more than able to heal you and lead you back to worship through the power of His Spirit who lives in you and marks you as not just legitimate, but His own. He is the real thing and wants you to have the real thing. He wants you to have Him. And those who seek Him do.

> "Ask, and it will be given to you. Seek, and you will find. Knock, and the door will be opened to you. For everyone who asks receives, and the one who seeks finds, and to the one who knocks, the door will be opened." (Matt. 7:7–8)

Chapter 3

Ham-hocking and Being Held

Grandma Marlene spent most of her life nestled away in Miami Shores. She collected plastic bags and shopping catalogs and paper clips, and stored all of her "treasures" neatly and meticulously. If you went over to visit, you could always expect to find a tray full of assorted goodies. She loved hosting. She loved loving people. And I was lucky enough to be her first-born granddaughter.

She took care of me a lot, growing up. And when she kept me at her house, we'd spend a lot of time outside. There were two trees in her backyard that were perfect for a hammock. Or a "ham-hock" as she used to call it. I never gave it a second thought, the times she pushed me back and forth, while I let my body relax completely, all my childhood cares whooshing away with every nudge of her hand.

She'd sing songs about Jesus and never seemed to tire of swinging me. With just over three years of heaven under her belt now, and who knows how many years since I used to swing, carefree, in her hammock, life has changed so much.

Now, I'm the one pushing my girls in hammocks. I'm the one singing them Jesus songs. I'm the one trying to remind them of our great hope, even as I struggle to remember I have it myself sometimes.

It's a weird change that happens, when you transition from being cared for to being the caretaker. You feel this new weight as an adult, when you've moved away from being cared for. The problem, at least where I stand, is that the longing to be cared for doesn't go away. I'm not a man, but I'm married to one, and there were a few that helped raise me, and I know from hearing their stories that the longing doesn't really go away for them either.

As we grow up, many of us acquire dependents, and then the people who used to take care of us either disappear by death or end up needing us to care for them. And doesn't the weight of the world feel heavier when that happens?

While I was still caught in the dizzying grief of losing Uncle Jimmy, I got a devastating call from the other side of the country, that Grandma Marlene had Covid and pneumonia, was in the hospital, and was saying her goodbyes.

There was no time to book a flight. There wasn't even time to buy a new grieving sweat suit at Target. I was in my car when I got that call, so I had to pull over at the nearest parking lot, which was an apartment complex by the Pacific Ocean in Corona del Mar.

The air was perfect that day. The sky was blue. The ocean was vast and beautiful. And it felt like my whole world was falling apart.

The person who pushed me in the ham-hock until my cares disappeared was going away for the rest of my life. How can that happen? The person who knew that I didn't like nuts in fudge, so every Christmas she'd make a separate few with no nuts, just for me—she was just going to be gone? While I was driving home past the ocean? It didn't compute.

Those days and weeks and months and first few years after her death, I tried to find substitutes for the comfort of Grandma. But nothing could replace the feeling of being held in her hammock, being lulled into peace by her voice—a voice I knew so well, a person who knew me so well. No food or drink or entertainment could fill that void she left.

So here's a frustrating layer to grieving as a Christian. We know the truth. In fact, I bet you know exactly what I'm about to say—something about how turning to Him instead of comfort-substitutes will solve our problems.

That is the last thing a cynical, hurting, grief-stricken person *wants* to hear, right? Because sometimes none of that *feels* true. Maybe you've spent years reading and praying and listening for God's voice, but aren't tangible voices of loved ones what we crave? The warm hug that feels like home. Sometimes it's hard to hope for that in the supernatural when you're in the midst of suffering. When God feels far away, or maybe even not real? Dare we even say that? Are we even allowed to feel it?

Those of us who have, in the past, tasted and seen that the Lord is good (Ps. 34:8) know that we ought to know better. But when our comforters die or leave or go away, we forget.

Being Cared for Through a Bible Reading Plan

God's people throughout recent and ancient history have always been forgetful. While we lived in California, I completed a task I'd always wanted to complete—to read the Bible straight through from beginning to end. Wonder of wonders, it took me five years. Now, you may be one of those Christians who enjoys an annual or bi-annual Bible reading plan and man, good for you. Seriously. I mean that. I have learned so much from you, the disciplined disciples of Jesus. Truthfully, I've always wanted to be more like you.

But for me, for so many years of my faith, I'd try to read the harder parts of the Old Testament, get confused, lost, or frustrated, and return back to my New Testament tried-and-true. I'd dabble in the Old, but I knew, even after years of dabbling, there were parts I'd missed, skipped over, or given up on.

So I told myself that no matter how long it would take, no matter what other Bible studies I may have signed up to do on the side, I was going read this little maroon Bible I had from cover to cover. I was going to learn God's voice and God's story in a way I never had.

And that experience really was life changing.

I'd been through twelve years of Christian school, four years of Christian college, and countless church Bible studies, but ingesting Scripture in its totality makes a lot click that just can't if you only skip around.

Those years I read the Bible that way, I was struck by just how sinful, forgetful, and frustrating God's people were in the early part of their story. I know I mentioned them in the last chapter. But man, have I identified with their failures and forgetfulness as I've walked through the sadness of the past few years.

Honestly, I used to envy the early people of God who got to see, hear, and experience God—whether it be witnessing a burning bush, receiving tablets God wrote with His own hand, or walking through a split sea. Fast-forward some years and I envied the same sorts of things that the disciples got to experience: knowing the lines of Jesus's face, His tone of voice, His encouragement and laughter. For those disciples, Jesus was as real as Grandma Marlene was to me. And still . . . Peter denied Him. Judas betrayed Him. Thomas doubted Him. And I suppose Jesus was used to it. Before He came to earth in human form, He was one with the Father. He was God's Son, there with God at the beginning and there when Israel kept losing all memory of heaven's faithfulness to them. For all the signs and wonders witnessed, Moses still failed God and the Israelites routinely worshipped other gods. Old Testament and New, the story is the same.

So how did God deal with them in their wanderings?

Sometimes, He allowed them to walk through the consequences of their sin. Sometimes, He sent miracles Sometimes He altered time and space and physics to communicate His power and His presence to them. And my goodness, did He show them mercy.

They'd trudge through their lives, grumbling and cursing and sinning and complaining, and He forgave and showed compassion again and again and again. His mercy healed their wounds and made them into more merciful people. And that's something I know God does for us, even when we hurt, even when we go silent, even when we doubt, even when we wander.

He shows mercy. He shows compassion. He alerts us of His presence. He proclaims His name to us all over again, and in doing so, reminds us of His nature. He stays true to what He says is core to who He is. In Moses's burning bush moment, God freshly introduced Himself. The encounter went something like this in the book of Exodus:

> Hello, Moses, if you're wondering who's talking to you out of this fiery bush, it is Me, God. "I am the God of your father, the God of Abraham, the God of Isaac and the God of Jacob." And just in case you're wondering why I'd appear right here and right now, it's because "I have indeed seen the misery of my people in Egypt. I have heard them crying out because of their slave drivers, and I am concerned about their suffering." And if you're wondering what I'm going to do about it, well, "I have come down to rescue them from the hand of the Egyptians." Also, an important point: I'd like you to be the guy who goes to the king of the Egyptians and tells him these

> things, demanding that he release My people from his terrible mastery over them. And in case you're nervous about that job description, don't worry, "I will be with you," and you can tell them that "I AM" sent you—meaning, Me, the One who has always existed and declares Himself not only as God of all creation, but by another name too: "Lord." Meaning, the deity with special jurisdiction over this specific people group, the Israelites, a covenant God who will never give up on them. (3:6–8, 12, 14–15 NIV)

This is a remarkable encounter between Moses and God, but knowing God's name—"The LORD"—isn't quite enough for Moses. Sure, this God has special jurisdiction over Israel, and sure, He seems to be showing interest in their suffering right this moment. But for what purpose? What if this "LORD" is going to bring them out of Egyptian slavery only to throw them right back into back-breaking labor and enslavement somewhere else? How can Moses know this "LORD" isn't short-tempered? What if this God has pity on the people now, but when they do something to cross Him or disobey Him, will He stay that way? Or will He turn on them and abandon them? How can Moses know this God is trustworthy—especially when attempting something so risky?

Thankfully, another part of Exodus clears up the matter. It shows us not just the Lord's *name*, but what this name *means* in regard to His long-term character:

> Then the LORD came down in the cloud and stood there with him and proclaimed his name, the LORD. And he passed in front of Moses, proclaiming, "The LORD, the LORD, the compassionate and gracious God, slow to anger, abounding in love and faithfulness, maintaining love to thousands, and forgiving wickedness, rebellion and sin." (Exod. 34:5–7 NIV)

As it turns out, when this God says "I will be with you" to Moses in his daunting, impossible, scary task, He doesn't mean some random, fickle, exacting God will be hovering over his shoulder. The one who will be with Moses from that point forward—the presence hovering over him during the terrifying and wonderful task in front of him—is the world's most compassionate, gracious, patient, loving, faithful, and forgiving Person in the world.

Can you think of a burning-bush sort of moment in your life? One where you were caught off guard by God interrupting your plans and asking you to do something you *know* you can't do? One where, somehow, at the same time, you were freshly re-introduced to God's mercy, presence, graciousness, and love? Talk about a double whammy.

Most recently, for me, it was a surprise baby I didn't plan on having as a thirty-eight-year-old, with three kids, the youngest being NINE.

Being Carried While Carrying Baby James

I signed the contract to write this book, *Hopeful-ish*, on January 26th.

I had a work trip to Minnesota that weekend, and I was grateful and excited to have a new writing project. Writing books has always been my favorite thing, ever since the third grade, when our teacher said we could spend free time filling the little white blank books on the bookshelves with our own stories. Every time I get to write a book again, it feels like a little miracle, and right there at the start of a new year, I had my plans laid out before me.

I had a bunch of trips scheduled for the spring, where I'd fly around with my nails done and my Starbucks in my hand and the sweet, quiet respites from homeschool mom life. I'd arrive in a new city and I'd tell women how wonderful Jesus has been in my life. I'd get to hug them and hear their stories and eat their favorite foods with them. Such a joy.

Then, I'd go back to my comfortable home with my sweet family and I'd leisurely type away. It was going to be a fun and fruitful year, involving doing the ministry I love, hanging out with my easy independent daughters, and being comfortable, after several years of sadness and discomfort.

God had slightly different plans for my year.

The weekend before I took the positive pregnancy test, Dewy, my youngest, the baby—almost nine at the time—saw a cute baby at church and said, "Mommy, can you *pulleeee-aaase* have one more baby . . ." And I responded, like I knew exactly what was going on with my body and future, "No, love, we're allllll done with babies in this family."

I'm pretty sure I saw a tired mom carrying her newborn into the church service that same day and said something like, "So cute! You must be so tired. Don't worry. You'll sleep again someday. I sleep great!"

Fa la la la la . . . doo do doo . . .

Five days later, the positive pregnancy test. What in the actual world?

I didn't even tell Brandon I was going to take a test. He's forty-two years old! I'm thirty-eight! The medical term genuinely, seriously is "geriatric pregnancy."

He walked into our bathroom and found me in shock. I don't think we even exchanged words. Later he told me he had figured out exactly what was going on because apparently I was "making a face [he'd] never seen before."

When I asked him to describe it, he said it was a mixture of shock, anger, and joy. I'm thirty-eight. I'm thirty-eight. Have I mentioned I'm *thirty-eight*?

Like I said, I'd just weeks earlier signed the contract to write this book—the idea birthed out of several years of suffering in my life—suffering that led to feeling hopelessness, cynicism, and settling into chasing comforts that don't really comfort. I was settling. I was following Jesus with a limp. So tired. So beat up.

God knew what I needed better than I did.

It's one thing to preach the gospel to yourself, to write out and share testimonies of truth and hope. But, it's another thing entirely to experience the jolt-force of a surprise new life

. . . the surrendering of your time and body and plans . . . the sickness and weakness and helplessness.

Thank You, Lord.

It's hard to stay cynical when you're looking into the face of a brand-new life, a brand-new soul that has experienced nothing but care and comfort. By the time you're reading this, Lord willing, I will be like those nursery moms at church, bleary-eyed and *not nauseated* and bouncing a new baby—rediscovering wonder and hope through the eyes of a tiny person who hasn't experienced heartache or disappointment or loss yet.

When God Interrupts Your Plans

Maybe thirty-eight is a little early to feel settled down, but I was fully in my rut, and I was loving it. I observed other women in the life stages I'd said farewell to, and did not envy their exhaustion, their busyness, or the dying-to-self that their life stage required.

It wasn't long after that pregnancy test that I remembered the reality of the months that turn to years where you, as a mother, feel like your body is no longer your own. Everything hurts, the heaving catches you off guard before you know it's coming, and the comfortable, approved activities that you had planned out in the calendar of your life are suddenly taken over. You are no longer able to believe the lie that you're in control of your life. You're no longer able to forget the reality that your life is not your own.

What a shock. What a gift.

This God-interruption I've been given this year has reminded me a little of when Jesus spoke with the disciples about denying themselves . . .

> Then Jesus said to his disciples, "If anyone wants to follow after me, let him deny himself, take up his cross, and follow me. For whoever wants to save his life will lose it, but whoever loses his life because of me will find it. For what will it benefit someone if he gains the whole world yet loses his life? Or what will anyone give in exchange for his life?" (Matt. 16:24–26)

I kind of can't believe how casually I was clocking my days, hunkering down, settling in, making peace, and making plans. The personal tragedies and the letdowns and pains had been whittling away at my joy and passion for life, and I was, often I think, mostly drifting, going through motions. Trying to avoid the pain. Trying to avoid reality, really.

How often did my life, pre-interruption, require denying my personal plans and feelings and desires? How costly did my faith feel? How familiar with reality was I, really?

But that's the thing about God. He helps us show back up to the real world. He helps us enter back into not only reality, but usually into a certain assignment within reality—an assignment that requires eyes wide open, heart poured out before Him, mind full of prayers and questions and praises and conundrums and truths. Or, in short, an assignment that requires a person fully alive to Him.

God's Sovereign Timing

The past few years of pain have felt like so much, too much. I'd been fighting to remember that my hope isn't dependent on how hopeful I am, but on the reality of the expectation of good Jesus secured for me with His finished work on the cross. Some days, getting there in my heart felt harder. That made it easy for me to slink away from serving sacrificially and joyfully.

But that's no way to live. Feeble, distracted, and barely hopeful.

God knew that. He knew that my plan this year was to rest and write and try to remember His goodness from the comfort of my home and that healthy, predictable body of mine. And I'm not saying He doesn't draw us into seasons of slowness and rest sometimes. But, in my case, and for what my own spiritual walk needed in this particular leg of the journey, what kind of faith would that have produced? What kind of growth might I have seen? Even without His sweet interruption, I trust God would have continued to transform me into His image with ever-increasing glory (2 Cor. 3:18), but I can't even tell you what a soul jump-start it's been to be surprised by this gift of a new baby. I was planning for what I wanted, but God gave me what I needed. Not only does He have plans for this baby to be alive in this world for His purposes, *I* also needed to be fully alive to God again instead of drifting away into spiritual oblivion, and this is the way God pulled off both feats.

I love being a mother to my three little girls. And now I get to do it again. The Lord, in His kindness, weakened my body and reminded me of my need for Him and dependence on Him in the most precious and glorious way. Like Moses, I have a new, appropriately heavy task. It *should* feel weighty, in a sense. But I'm not alone in it. I'm alive to the One who says "I will be with you" throughout the journey of not just birth, but the two decades of raising this child on the other side. And this "I"—this "LORD" I claim as my own—is just as compassionate, gracious, patient, loving, faithful, and forgiving as He was for Moses. He's interrupted me, yes. But He has interrupted me with more than merely a heavy task ahead of me. He's interrupted me with *Himself.* And by waking me up and driving me to Himself, I'm more alive and engaged in faith now than I have been in years.

I don't know what burning bush moment you have in your life right now, what interruption feels impossible. But I can promise you this: If you fully lean into the gift that it is, you'll discover not only the glorious beauty and privilege of the task itself, but you'll discover more of God, and more of yourself along the way too.

Right Where He Wants Us

I feel so undeserving of this gift. Even with the morning sickness, the exhaustion, and the intense discomfort I'm feeling as I write this, I am stunned and humbled that God would wake me up from my coasting in such a kind way. Thank You, God, for reminding me that my life is not my own. Thank

You, Father, for leading me to focus on how I can serve, not just how I can sit. Thank You, Lord, for reawakening me to the reality that You want to use me beyond the plans I make for myself. Thank You, I am—the God who is alive and existent compared to the impotent and dead gods of this world—for bringing people like me back to life in the most unexpected ways when they'd rather just numb out and disappear.

I pray God gives you a fresh opportunity to remember His power and sufficiency and the fruit He wants to bear through your life. Maybe your jolt won't be a "geriatric" pregnancy. But, if you look closely at your life, I'm certain you'll see God's kindness leading you to repentance and renewal over and over again.

> Or do you despise the riches of his kindness, restraint, and patience, not recognizing that God's kindness is intended to lead you to repentance? (Rom. 2:4)

Maybe you're sitting on the couch in your clean house with a candle lit right now, feeling a little uncomfortable with your current level of comfort. I think I'd gotten so comfortable in comfort-seeking that I was losing my desire to press in, to obey when it's hard, to serve in secret.

I know God has many other strategies besides surprise babies to remind His followers of their purpose and the joy available to them by living on mission. I know from past experience that He uses words from friends, hymns at church, and even random paragraphs in the middle of random books to remind His children that obedience leads to joy and that the comfort He gives is bottomless and always available.

I barely worked on this book at all in my first trimester. I mostly laid in bed, squinting in pain, moaning, preparing to or recovering from throwing up. It was physical misery, and my life felt completely non-productive. The house was a mess, my emotions were a mess.

You'd think my feeling-the-weight-of-the-world problem would be intensified, but weirdly, the opposite happened. There's something about life getting so out of control feeling, that you just kind of . . . *have to* lean into the feeling of powerlessness, you know?

And when we find that we are powerless, we are ready to rely on the One who is powerful. Sure, when you grow up, you move away from being cared for and find yourself as the caretaker still longing for someone to nurture you. But the thing is, there is Someone who wants to nurture you, Someone able to wipe your tears, and help you look past your loss and your pain to the beautiful inheritance He has for you. This is the Lord who promises "I will go with you," who showers mercy on you, forgives you, loves you, remains faithful to you, and guides you through the hard and the deep and the impossible, just as He did with Moses.

How He Does It

It probably sounds nice to hear that the same "Lord" who led Moses through his hard, deep, impossible task will lead you through whatever interruptions come your way. But if you're anything like me, you start asking questions. Questions like, *How? I mean, that was thousands of years ago. And I don't see waters parting or manna falling from heaven in my darkest moments. How can this God still be around? How can I know this "LORD" isn't the same as Grandma Marlene—sweet and able to help in a certain season, but gone after a while? How can I know He won't fade on me?*

My husband frequently preaches a heady sermon about God, as Creator, using big philosophical words. He talks about God as our "Uncaused Cause." And when I say "talks" I mean all the time. He's preached about this in so many sermons and in so many cities that I've started teasing him about how often the "Uncaused Cause" comes out of his mouth. Many Sundays, I'll joke, "Are we going to get to hear about the Uncaused Cause again today? (I'm not kidding when I say, he once found a way to work the Uncaused Cause into a family funeral.)

But that's because it *is* important.

The cosmological argument for the existence of God says this, essentially: Everything that has (or had) a beginning has a cause. And you can trace causes back one by one. Z exists because something earlier caused it: Y. But Y only exists because something prior caused it, and that's X. You can trace it back all the way to point A, but then the natural question becomes, well, what caused A to begin with? How did A burst into being? Children everywhere work through this line of reasoning when they ask how Mommy and Daddy got here (and if they are anything like my kids, they'll try to trace the family line all the way back to Adam and Eve for hours on end instead of going to bed). If this cause-stuff is true, then the universe itself, which scientists agree had a beginning, has a cause—and that's God. God is the original cause—the Uncaused Causer. He's where the buck must stop because nothing caused Him. There's no prior thing before Him that could have burst Him into being. So it always comes back to John 1.

> In the beginning was the Word, and the Word was with God, and the Word was God. He was with God in the beginning. All things were created through him, and apart from him not one thing was created that has been created. *In him was life,* and that life was the light of men. (vv. 1–4, emphasis added)

God is the Uncaused Causer of everything. Why does this matter? Because of that one little phrase in italics above: "In him was LIFE." This is where all life comes from. The universe's life, Mommy and Daddy's life, the life of any living creature. If we trace any living thing backward, we end up with Him, the life-giving God.

This is the very reason you can trust that the same God who helped Moses can help you. It's the very reason you can trust that the God who helped the disciples and even me, the author of this book, will still be around for your next set of assignments, interruptions, and trials. It's the very reason you can bank on the fact that this "LORD" isn't the same as Grandma Marlene—great as she was. Because there's no such thing as "gone after a while" with God. He is life itself. He cannot fade on you because He's alive, right now, guiding you and helping you and comforting you and interrupting you with His good plans, readying you for true rest on the other side of glory, where He'll grant you not just earthly life, but eternal, resurrected life. Forever.

Said another way, we have life because God created it. We have a future because God promises it. We have hope—*"right now"* hope as I phrased it in the last chapter—because Jesus suffered and died for it. We can rest in the care and comfort and nurturing of our Father because not only does He only do good, not only does He know the number of hairs on our head (Luke 12:7), but as we learned in the last chapter, *He is alive.* Forever alive.

Grandma Marlene died. I don't get to be nurtured by her anymore. Today, taking my kids to school, I drove past her old neighborhood—the place she used to reside—knowing that if I were to pull into her driveway, there might be new people living there, but there would be no Mini Coop. There would be no snack tray. There would be no Grandma.

And God died too, in the person of Christ. But then He came back to life. And He promises to resurrect His saints. This means when we come upon Jesus's throne room—the place He resides—we need not fear we won't see evidence of Him any longer. We won't find an empty chair, or someone else who moved in. He's there, seated, available, and involved. Living and breathing, just like us.

That's good news for a weary believer like me. Interruptions are part of the deal on this side of heaven. They are important. As our Living God leads us through them, they not only help wake us up in this life, they ready us for our eternal future, where instead numbing out forever and ever amen, we'll rest with God and each other the right way.

A Final Interruption and a Glorious Future

I'll leave you with these verses from 1 Thessalonians 4, because it's a great reminder of the final, glorious interruption this world will experience when Jesus cracks the sky open and returns. The heading in my Bible says, "The Comfort of Christ's Coming."

> We do not want you to be uninformed, brothers and sisters, concerning those who are asleep, so that you will not grieve like the rest, who have no hope. For if we believe that Jesus died and rose again, in the same way, through Jesus, God will bring with him those who have fallen asleep. For we say this to you by a word from the Lord: We who are still alive at the Lord's coming will certainly not precede those who have fallen asleep. For the Lord himself will descend from heaven with a shout, with the archangel's voice, and with the trumpet of God, and the dead in Christ will rise first. Then we who are still alive, who are left, will be caught up together with them in the clouds to meet the Lord in the air, and

> so we will always be with the Lord. Therefore encourage one another with these words. (1 Thess. 4:13–18)

Encourage one another with these words. It's been a long time since I've been in Grandma's "ham-hock" or her squishy, tight embrace. But God says I don't have to grieve that loss as one who has no hope. God says that just as Jesus died and rose again, so will Grandma. And so will I. After we get through all the interruptions of this life, we will meet the Lord in the air and always be with Him, the Lord of Life. The One who was not only with us every step of the way, but proved Himself a good guide. And He will be the One pushing the hammock. And we will all get to rest together.

We will be held and we will be home.

Chapter 4

"Wow . . . You Have NONE Friends."

When we first moved to California, we were living in Airbnbs and after a few weeks, our youngest daughter bounced into the room with a question for Dad.

"Daddy? How many friends have you made since we moved?"

"I don't think I've made any friends yet, Beauty," he said.

"Wow . . ." she said, looking both shocked and sympathetic, ". . . You have NONE friends."

Funny. But, as most truly funny things are, also sad. Leading up to our California-bound move, we'd just walked through a lot of relationship loss.

Weirdly, the relational loss has continued, here in 2024 as I write. Brandon and I have both, in our pain, asked the Lord why He's allowed us to see so many loved ones move away. We both know that any painful thing the Lord allows draws us into a closer dependence on Him, but we also know that He made us to live and thrive in Christian community. So experiencing such a long string of losses was a little confusing.

It started during the best year of our lives—2018. Brandon usually had a cartoonish spring in his step every day when he got home from work because he felt so fulfilled by the ministry he was a part of, and was working with people he loved and respected. I was also high on life, as I'd just signed my first publishing contract and was writing the book I'd been dreaming of writing since third grade. We'd just adopted our middle daughter from China, and she was healing and thriving and doing amazing. And our biological girls were wonderful as could be. We were truly living a charmed life.

But the most beautiful part of it all was our church community. Brandon was an elder at our bustling, fast-growing church, and there were about three families we did everything with. The pastor and his family were, "Hey, it's been a few days. Can we come sit around the firepit with you tonight after dinner?" type of friends. Our kids were besties and we had people in our corner. Loneliness was not part of our vocabulary. Life was full and happy and busy and beautiful.

And then, our people started disappearing. It was crazy.

The vice president of Brandon's company moved across the country to go back into full-time pastoral ministry. He and his wife were mentors/friends/frien-tors to us and it was hard to see them go. A few months later, our pastor and his family moved away. Our closest family friends, gone.

Then, another family we loved and did life with moved to literal Japan.

After our pastor left, our church went through some changes that led us to believing we needed to step away. So within a year, we found that the beautiful, robust life we'd built had been stripped away. Our farm was empty. We found ourselves church shopping after years of assuming we'd always and forever get to do life with the people we'd been serving with.

We floundered for a bit, but then figured that God had allowed all the relational loss to prepare us for an Isaiah 6 type of "Here I am, send me," moment.

Meanwhile, Covid burst onto the scene, changing the planet, and of course leading to even more loss . . . layoffs that affected close friends, sickness that led to deaths.

We ended up in California, which felt like an extended mission trip. The girls and I forged some friendships, but Brandon struggled to settle. He worked constantly, and we ended up feeling very far from home.

So we moved back, and I've already told you how well that went.

Brandon's job changed. And as I've already mentioned, his close friends invited him to goodbye lunches. His family came and went back to South Carolina. And once again, our pastor moved away. A different pastor. Of a different church.

But this time, we were middle-aged, with far less "starting over" energy. And we were as "back home" as we could hope to be. But it didn't feel like home anymore. Instead, we found ourselves lonely on a *different* farm, only twenty minutes away from our first one.

So what is it that God is doing when He lets our people leave?

If you're looking to me and this book for the answer, don't worry. I'm going to Google it. Please hold.

Craig's Answer vs. Google's Answer

Well, reader. I looked into it. And unfortunately, Google did not provide any satisfactory explanations for the relational heartaches of the Hiltibidals.

Instead, I'll tell you what my husband's friend, Craig, told him. They were out at lunch and Brandon was just walking him through all the goodbyes and disappointments of the last few years, and Craig encouraged him never to play the *What-if* game.

He reminded Brandon that God's ways are higher than our ways.

> "For my thoughts are not your thoughts, and your ways are not my ways." This is the Lord's declaration. "For as heaven is higher than earth, so my ways are higher than your ways, and my thoughts than your thoughts." (Isa. 55:8–9)

Craig reminded Brandon that there is no telling what sort of trouble our sovereign, all-knowing, all-powerful God had protected our family from in an uncomfortable way. In short, Craig preached the wisdom of God in a Mexican restaurant in a way that Google can't.

If we really are like children and God really is not just a more knowing but a perfectly knowing and perfectly good Father, that means we can trust Him even when we don't understand. In fact, we need to trust Him especially when we don't understand. Listen to this quote from John Newton (that

I heard from Tim Keller). "Everything is necessary that God sends our way; nothing can be necessary that he withholds."[6] This is a beautiful and painful truth that should shape our sense of what hope should be. His ways are higher.

One of my three currently-out-of-the-womb children questions my commands pretty frequently. It can be very frustrating, as a mom, and can definitely lead one to understand the age-old classic mom response—"Because I said so."

It's frustrating because I know better than she does. I know the reason behind the simple commands I give.

"Let's use markers at the table, not on the white blanket."

"Hey, sweetie, it's time to shower before we have snuggle time in Mommy's bed."

"Make sure you wear your phone-watch before you go out into the field to feed the animals."

I don't have to tell you, reader, the *why* behind those commands. They're obvious, right? I don't want a stained blanket. I don't want sweaty kid feet in my sheets. I want my girls to be safe and have a way to contact me if they are out of eyeshot and earshot, so I can keep them safe in case a donkey charges at them out of nowhere. Reasonable commands, right?

But when said child questions my commands, or even worse, disobeys because she thinks her way is a better way, it drives me crazy. I feel a valid and justified frustration bubble up . . . *She doesn't know what I know. I've been alive so many more years than she has. I don't owe her an explanation! And also, when is this whole thing going to catch on? When is she going to start being respectful? When will she just trust me, for crying out loud?*

The space between my children and me? A couple of decades. The space between humans and God? Light-years. It's bizarre to think about how God must feel when we question why He allowed certain things or certain people to come into or go out of our lives. Amazingly, we do get to see some of this emotion in the Bible, in His response to the Israelites, to Moses, to Job, and on and on.

We have no right to question God, and yet He has compassion and mercy when we do.

The apostle Paul addresses this in Romans 9:

> . . . who are you, a human being, to talk back to God? Will what is formed say to the one who formed it, "Why did you make me like this?" Or has the potter no right over the clay, to make from the same lump one piece of pottery for honor and another for dishonor? And what if God, wanting to display his wrath and to make his power known, endured with much patience objects of wrath prepared for destruction? And what if he did this to make known the riches of his glory on objects of mercy that he prepared beforehand for glory? (vv. 20b–23)

That is a heavy, difficult few verses there, isn't it? It feels uncomfortable to be the clay, the child, the created one who is not in control, right?

So then, how kind, that our just God would converse with us, as He did with His people in the Old Testament. How kind and miraculous that we can tell Him our feelings, our thoughts, our requests . . . and He hears us and responds personally? How surprising is it that instead of shooing us away, He *instructs* us to pour out our heavy hearts to Him (Ps. 62:8)? How compassionate is it that He gets frustrated when we *don't* consult Him with our many questions (Isa. 30:2)?

I want to be so much more like Him as a parent than I am. I want my children to obey and respect me, but I want to show compassion and understanding in their questioning.

I told my questioner this afternoon, "You have to obey when Mommy gives you a command. You have to obey, because you know that I love you and know better than you do. Even if you don't understand or don't agree, you have to obey. But if you've already obeyed respectfully, and then have questions, you can ask your questions. It's just important that you obey, first."

Now, let's be clear: This isn't a parenting book. This isn't even a parenting chapter. This chapter is about the pain of life and the sovereignty of God.

But I think that if we're going to look to someone for how to care for and love our people well, we should look to God.

We want to do it all right, and often we fail. But God always does right. And when I look at Scripture, I see a God who is holy and just, but who also made Himself human. I see a God who listens to His people now, and listened to His people since the beginning, even when His people had questions.

- Moses asked, "Why have you dealt ill with your servant?" (Num. 11:11 ESV).

- Elijah cried out to the LORD, "Why have you brought tragedy to this widow who has opened her home to me?" (1 Kings 17:20 NLT).
- David asked, "Why, LORD, do you stand far off? Why do you hide yourself in times of trouble?" (Ps. 10:1 NIV).
- Habakkuk asked, "Why do you force me to look at injustice? Why do you tolerate wrongdoing?" (Hab. 1:3).
- Job asked, "Why have you made me your target?" (Job 7:20).
- The disciples asked, "Why was this man born blind?" (John 9:2 NLT).
- Jesus on the cross asked God, "My God, my God, why have you forsaken me?" (Matt. 27:46 NIV).

Maybe some of your questions for God sound like, "Why did You do that, God? Why did You let that job slip through my fingers? Why did You let those people leave me? Why was that friend offended by me, when I don't think I was being offensive?"

Whether it's the Bible's list of questions or our own, we have a God who welcomes them.

Resisting False Hope and False Happiness in Isolation

I tend toward isolation. To me, it mostly feels peaceful and positive. Loneliness has been such a rare feeling for me, because when you long for the absence of friction and find it in limited human contact, it's hard to complain.

I don't think I ever uttered the words "I'm lonely" or even had them in my mind as a passing thought until my late thirties, when I'd experienced enough of the beauty of community to know that God's way is the best way and we really were made to hold each other up and help each other to Jesus.

Many of my friendship losses in life have been due to the fact that, since birth, I've been moving around the country like it's my job. I often identify with military families in this way. A few years ago, I was in a Bible study being led by a beautiful, blue-eyed military wife, Lauren. She was proactive in setting up playdates and coffee dates and we got to know each other quickly. The first time we hung out she explained that because of her husband's military commitments, she'd probably only be around for about three years. I think she actually moved away sooner than that, but we still loosely keep in touch.

I don't have a military husband as a reason, but because of my upbringing, my stays in cities have often been shorter than longer. New York, Connecticut, Los Angeles, Miami, Vancouver, Los Angeles, Miami, etc.

Turning new leaves and finding new friends has always been a happy thing for me, as the longer you know someone, the greater chance conflict can arise.

But, here in the late thirties, I thank God for the friends I have that have endured moves and even conflicts. Those relationships are so much richer and more meaningful than the fun, new, easy, surfacey ones.

When I'm dealing with a real struggle, a real problem, I don't want to talk to a new friend, whom I'd have to fill in on thirty-eight years of information in order for them to have the context and understanding they'd need to be able to grasp the pain I'm going through. No. If I have a real struggle, I want to talk to Katie. Katie has seen me through more than twelve years of happy moments and heartaches. We've had enough front porch and phone conversations that she knows the name, personality, and history of every extended family member I have, and vice versa.

If I say, "So-and-so distant relative called," Katie knows what that means. She knows whether to rejoice with me or cry with me. If I say, "I'm struggling," she usually knows whether she should say something comforting or convicting. When you walk with someone through the years, it gets easier to see the difference between sadness and sin. And it is easier to lean in with real love. What is better than having a Katie?

And it goes both ways. I know her. I know about her brothers and their wives. I know about her kids and their family business and their vacations. I'm able to be there for her in ways others can't, because she's let me into the day-to-day of her life for so long.

Before having a friend like Katie, I really didn't know what I was missing out on. In crisis, I'd go to a counselor, and of course have to spend a handful of sessions giving them a personal history, so they might have some insight into my life. Counselors are great, and have helped me so many times, but there's nothing like a Katie.

Because Katie has known excited me and tired me and depressed me and hermit me. She's stuck around. She knows. What a gift.

But I've had other friends that I thought might be Katie-level, who wound up fading away. In some of those situations, I could clearly find my failure in it. I think back to a college friendship that I ruined. I talked about her behind her back with a mutual friend. It got back to her, and the truth is, I was just plain guilty. She didn't trust me anymore, and I understood. But there are other losses that left me confused and feeling exposed. One of the great heartaches of my lifetime was having a very close friend, a friend I felt I could be my full true vulnerable self with. Then later on, I learned that the way I talked, lived, and functioned simply wasn't her favorite. In that situation, it turned out, the offense was more *how I am* than something I did.

I felt so misunderstood. I did apologize to that friend, because she was hurt by me, whether or not I understood how or agreed with the assessment. (One thing I've learned in life is that in most conflicts, there's usually *something* you can own in whatever went wrong, and I wanted to offer that.) But I left our conversation near the end so hurt and confused, not knowing how I could have done any of it differently. I knew

I wasn't innocent, as all humans say and do stupid and selfish things. But I felt that she didn't know my heart or give me the benefit of the doubt.

I was in counseling, talking through that situation for a long time. I told my counselor, I just wanted to feel good about the relationship, in hindsight. Even though we weren't in each other's lives anymore, I wanted some sort of closure. But I think the kind of relationship loss that hurts most is the kind that leaves you feeling wounded, misunderstood, and solutionless.

Years after that relationship ended, I told my counselor, "I just don't know how to be vulnerable with people now. To do life with someone for years and years, feel accepted and safe, only to learn you weren't . . . what do you do with that?" Then, I told her, when I'm haunted by that specific friendship wound, it triggers a process where I'll double down on it, scanning my history all the way back through middle school, digging up all painful relationships that I didn't know how to save. And at that point, I just spiral, I told her, feeling more broken and more damaged than the people I see around me.

I remember my counselor saying, "It sounds like you want to tie a bow on every loss. And the problem with that is, in life, you can't tie a bow on everything. You have to make peace with the fact that while it's always a good idea to at least try and reconcile with people on the other side of conflict, there are unresolved pains that will never be fixed in this life."

That was a weirdly comforting statement.

And I think it can be applied to sadness and grief of all kinds. In this life, I will never be able to tie a bow around the way my uncle died, or around why certain relationships ended. There are no tidy endings to famine and war. But not only does the Lord offer to carry our burdens and heartaches, He gives us the gift of real, gospel-infused, life-giving relationships, if we open ourselves up to them.

What I'm saying is this: Don't let the losses lead you to isolation. There's a false sense of security in being relationshipless. Cast your cares on the Lord and let Him sustain you through His presence and through the power of His Spirit in other believers.

> Cast your burden on the LORD, and he will sustain you. (Ps. 55:22a)

Invisible Friendship

Some of the most powerful ways I've seen and experienced Jesus have absolutely been through His followers. But a personal, intimate, one-on-one in the middle of the night thing with Jesus has held me together during the seasons I've felt most alone.

If you've been married for any length of time, you will know that disappointing feeling you have sometimes, when you're in some sort of pain and longing to connect with your spouse, but the way they respond to your feelings proves that they can't really get it. They can't fully know you. There is no person or counselor or app algorithm that can know you as deeply as Jesus—the God who made you and formed you and is able to see your thoughts.

The beautiful truth of Psalm 139 comes to mind, when I think about "what a friend I have in Jesus," to quote an old hymn my Grandma Marlene used to sing all the time. David wrote, "LORD, you have searched me and known me. You know when I sit down and when I stand up; you understand my thoughts from far away" (Ps. 139:1–2).

I love that David didn't just say "You know my thoughts . . ."

I feel like I do a pretty decent job of sharing my thoughts with my husband. He knows them. He doesn't doubt how I feel about things, good or bad, because I let him know. Sometimes, I let him know many times in a row, as repeating things is often part of "my process." (I might feel like Brandon knows my thoughts, but I often feel like he doesn't *understand* them. Thus, the repetitions.)

But God doesn't just know. He doesn't just hear me. He understands me. He doesn't just know about you; He gets you. He made our brains, after all. And we don't need to repeat any dramatic soliloquies to Him. We don't even need to think them.

God knows. He just knows. No disclaimers or certain turns of phrases or nuances or backstory needed. He simply understands. Better than we do.

One of the most comforting realities of a friendship with God, to me, is that I don't have to explain anything. Sometimes I can't. Even still, He knows and understands. He gets us when we can't even get the words out. He intercedes for us when we don't know what to say. How incredible is that?

> In the same way the Spirit also helps us in our weakness, because we do not know what to pray for as we should, but the Spirit himself intercedes for us with inexpressible groanings. And he who searches our hearts knows the mind of the Spirit, because he intercedes for the saints according to the will of God. (Rom. 8:26–27)

"In our weakness." "He intercedes." "He who searches our hearts." "Intercedes for the saints according to the will of God." Sing it again, Marlene. "What a friend we have in Jesus."

When I travel around and speak, I'm often there to share my testimony and how I've learned to battle my anxieties with the Word of God. In one part of my message, I always go through a bunch of Scripture that I have hung up around my house and sticky-noted to the back of my iPad—Scriptures that remind me of who Jesus is and who I am in Him. When I'm on stage, I like to read the Scripture and have a sort of audience participation thing where the crowd will tell me what that passage says about who they are in Jesus.

The verses I share lead the women to shout things like, "Approved!" "Loved!" "Forgiven!"

And then I always tell them, before I read the last two verses, "If I'm allowed to have a favorite, this is my favorite reality about who we are in Jesus," and then I read the following two verses:

> And the Scripture was fulfilled that says, "Abraham believed God, and it was credited

> to him as righteousness," and he was called God's friend. (James 2:23)

> So now we can rejoice in our wonderful new relationship with God because our Lord Jesus Christ has made us friends of God. (Rom. 5:11 NLT)

And then I point out at the crowd, and they shout, "Friend!"

What a blessing to get to be a friend of God. God is the only friend who can *literally* read your mind. "In our weakness." "He intercedes." He's the only friend who can intercede with the Father, asking things you don't even know to ask, on your behalf.

I'm enormously pregnant as I write this chapter, and this friendship-with-God reality reminds me of a conversation I keep having with my husband. I've been so uncomfortable throughout this pregnancy and I can't tell you how many times I've told Brandon, "I need . . . something. Can you . . . help? Bring me something?"

He responds, "What do you want?"

"I . . . don't know."

"Okay . . . I can't help you if you don't tell me what you want."

You know when it's too hard to even think about or decide what you want? Guess what? "In our weakness." "He intercedes." More than that, He knows what we need and what will ultimately comfort and fulfill and grow us. And He does that work for us. The Spirit talks to God for us. He takes our silence or our groanings or our wrong-sounding prayers and He translates them. Because He *understands*.

In Psalm 139, David continues:

> You observe my travels and my rest;
> you are aware of all my ways.
> Before a word is on my tongue,
> you know all about it, LORD.
> You have encircled me;
> you have placed your hand on me. (vv. 3–5)

If you read through the Old Testament and look through the life of David, you'll see some pretty major failures. David, God's friend, "a man after God's own heart" (1 Sam. 13:14), was an adulterer . . . who then had the husband of his mistress (a warrior in his own army) killed after he'd impregnated said mistress. These are not good things. These are not *friend-ish* things. Way before David, God had given His people a whopping 613 laws to obey. Laws about little things. But then, of course, there were the Ten Commandments, several of which involved David's indiscretions.

Don't murder . . . don't commit adultery . . . don't covet . . .

And our all-knowing, future-seeing God knew all the ways in which David would fail Him when He called David to Himself. So this just goes to reinforce the truth we see all over the Bible—that our friendship with God is not about our performance or our goodness. In the biggest ways . . . "In our weakness." "He intercedes."

Remember that verse about Abraham a couple pages ago?

> And the Scripture was fulfilled that says, "Abraham believed God, and it was credited to him as righteousness," and he was called God's friend. (James 2:23)

Abraham wasn't viewed by God as righteous because of his record of good works. It was because he "believed God." It was his faith. His faith absolutely led to faithful, often obedient good works. And sometimes it didn't. But his security in the Lord was because of what he believed about God, not because of what he did for God.

Even Abraham didn't always perfectly believe or respond to God in hope. God told him, in his old age, that he'd bear a son. And because God didn't seem to be coming through on the right timetable, he slept with his wife's slave and impregnated her. There is so much wrong with that last sentence. Those are not righteous actions and in that moment in his life, Abraham did not seem like a very "believing" person, right? The actions of someone who is walking in faith and obedience would be so opposite that.

Remembering these massive failures of these big time Bible heroes is so comforting to me. It's so reassuring. These friends of God were SO friends that they are talked about in the New Testament, in Hebrews 11, commended for their faith and faithful actions.

> By faith Abraham, when he was called, obeyed and set out for a place that he was going to

> receive as an inheritance. He went out, even though he did not know where he was going. By faith he stayed as a foreigner in the land of promise, living in tents as did Isaac and Jacob, coheirs of the same promise. For he was looking forward to the city that has foundations, whose architect and builder is God. By faith even Sarah herself, when she was unable to have children, received power to conceive offspring, even though she was past the age, since she considered that the one who had promised was faithful. Therefore, from one man—in fact, from one as good as dead—came offspring as numerous as the stars of the sky and as innumerable as the grains of sand along the seashore. . . .
>
> And what more can I say? Time is too short for me to tell about Gideon, Barak, Samson, Jephthah, David, Samuel, and the prophets, who by faith conquered kingdoms, administered justice, obtained promises, shut the mouths of lions, quenched the raging of fire, escaped the edge of the sword, gained strength in weakness, became mighty in battle, and put foreign armies to flight. . . . All these were approved through their faith . . . (Heb. 11:8–12, 32–34, 39a)

Abraham and Sarah and David had shining moments of faith in their lives and they had glaring moments of failure.

Don't we all want to be remembered for our shining moments? Our social-media-worthy snapshots?

How beautiful, then, that because of the goodness and sacrifice of Jesus, that is our reality when it comes to our status and friendship with God. Psalm 103, another psalm written by David, shows that he understood this.

> As far as the east is from the west,
> so far has he removed
> our transgressions from us. (v. 12)

In a world where relationships are so often conditional, what a comfort, what a gift, that God's love, God's friendship, isn't. If you find yourself in a moment where you have "none" friends, remind your hopeful-ish heart that you have a friend in Jesus. When He is yours and you are His, you are never alone. You are never unseen. He experienced true loneliness and true separation so that we would never have to. "And surely I am with you always, to the very end of the age," He says (Matt. 28:20 NIV). Believe it. "I no longer call you servants, because a servant does not know his master's business," He says, "Instead, I have called you *friends*, for everything that I learned from my Father I have made known to you" (John 15:15 NIV, emphasis added). Take hope.

The sadness that comes with friendship loss in this life is to be expected. But we can rejoice in our friendship with God, even during seasons when we feel alone. Sadness is natural. But hope in the midst of sadness is a supernatural gift, from our perfect, never-leaving, always-loving Friend. "In our weakness." "He intercedes."

Section 2

Weariness Is Inevitable, but Overcomable

"Come to me, all of you who are weary and burdened, and I will give you rest. Take my yoke upon you and learn from me, because I am lowly and humble in heart, and you will find rest for your souls."

Matthew 11:28–29

Chapter 5

Preteen Retirement Goals

My girls love to visit Grandma Mattie Lou (a.k.a. "Granny") in her assisted living facility. One of the great gifts of moving back to Tennessee was that it meant moving back to the Granny zone. Granny is gentle and fragile and sweet and easy to be around, and as I'm writing this, she just celebrated ninety years. Ninety.

We recently sat down on her couch and asked her what her weekly routine looked like, and she went through all of the activities and amenities available in her facility, and which were her favorite. With every mention of a new activity . . . education hour, Bible study, Bingo . . . my seventh grader's eyes grew wider and wider.

Then she said what she says every time we visit Granny, "I wish I could live in a retirement home."

A few minutes later, my parents arrived and we giggled about my preteen already daydreaming about retirement. She gushed, "There are puzzles and game nights and a cafeteria and friends everywhere and you have a home inside a building and the carpet smells so good and I just want to live here!"

We reminded her that what she was describing sounded exactly like college, and that's probably a more suitable thing to look forward to, but she disagreed. "No . . . college dorms aren't as nice and you have to work too hard."

True.

What my seventh grader was expressing in that moment was a longing for a life of ease. I don't know if you remember seventh grade, but I kind of think it might be the hardest one. The jump from the cozy, colorful repetition of elementary school to the cruel harsh reality of weekly essays and foreign language translations and "Blue Book Tests." It's a whole new world. And to my reeling middle schooler, a retirement home looked like *the life*.

Do you ever feel that? I sure do. After the past few years of heartache after heartache, exhaustion led me to chase comfort and rest like never before.

My ambition of years passed felt laughable, as my goals started shifting from *achieve this* and do that to . . . rest.

I know I'm not alone in this.

I've been traveling to different cities around the country to talk about Jesus for the past seven years, and every city I travel to, when I get face time with the women there, they echo the same things . . . *Life is sad . . . we're tired . . . where's the rest and how can I have it?*

Choosing Suffering over Ease

When Jesus came here, He did the opposite of what we often want to do. He *left* a place of perfect comfort, perfect peace, perfect rest, and traded it for *here.* He traded it to step into the mess we made.

He pursued the opposite of what we pursue, in order to secure, for us, the peace we long for on a soul-deep level. How often do you think about that? I know I don't think about it enough. Most of us spend so much of our time and brain space trying to trade up. We want to eliminate discomfort and trade it for all the good stuff.

Early in my faith, when I was trying to sort things out, I feared that godliness meant an actual desire for suffering. Like, *In order to really be like Jesus, I must want to live a life of poverty and suffering and pain.*

I spent a lot of those years overlooking the work of the Spirit in the life of a believer and ignoring the reality that Jesus's original creation, prior to being tainted by sin, *did* include blessing and abundance. It's not wrong to desire those things. We were created in the image of God, the source of all wholeness and happiness.

The problem isn't the desire for rest or wholeness. The problem is that sin broke the world and had to be dealt with. Jesus didn't come here because of some masochistic tendency; He came because of love. He came because those He *so loved* had a need that only He could meet, and the only way He could meet it was through His own suffering.

What this means for us is that following Jesus sometimes does get uncomfortable. Jesus made Himself uncomfortable and then told us to follow Him in kind:

> Then Jesus said to his disciples, "If anyone wants to follow after me, let him deny himself, take up his cross, and follow me. For whoever wants to save his life will lose it, but whoever loses his life because of me will find it." (Matt. 16:24–25)

I can definitely think back on times I tried to serve the Lord in an uncomfortable way, and it ended up feeling like it backfired; but more often than not, I feel like I'm on the receiving end of a gift. Even when it isn't easy, there is beauty in denying self and serving through the power of the Holy Spirit.

What Jesus Says to the Weary

Matthew 11 begins with doubt. John the Baptist, who had prepared the way for the coming of the Messiah, heard from prison that Jesus was preaching and he sent Jesus a message asking, "Are you the one who is to come, or should we expect someone else?" (v. 3b). A lot of people expected *someone else* when Jesus entered the picture. The Savior they probably pictured was strong and impressive and mighty. Think about the Jesus of the second coming. I remember that '90s church song, "Awesome God"—the one that talks about fire in His eyes and lightning in His fist. I think a lot of the Jews were expecting that same sort of Jesus—the one from Revelation 19:

> Then I saw heaven opened, and there was a white horse. Its rider is called Faithful and

> True, and with justice he judges and makes war. His eyes were like a fiery flame, and many crowns were on his head. He had a name written that no one knows except himself. He wore a robe dipped in blood, and his name is called the Word of God. The armies that were in heaven followed him on white horses, wearing pure white linen. A sharp sword came from his mouth, so that he might strike the nations with it. He will rule them with an iron rod. He will also trample the winepress of the fierce anger of God, the Almighty. And he has a name written on his robe and on his thigh: KING OF KINGS AND LORD OF LORDS. (vv. 11–16)

But, at the *first* coming, Jesus came humbly, almost quietly. Early in His ministry, He spoke in puzzles, so some could understand who He was and what He was saying. You have to remember Jewish people studied the Old Testament seriously. They'd heard the prophecies and were looking for the hero with the forever kingdom who was going to come make their lives better. But Jesus was born to no-name parents. He grew up in a backwater neighborhood—Nazareth. In John 1, we see Phillip telling Nathanial the good news—that the long-awaited Messiah has finally come. Nathaniel's response? So short-sighted and fallen. "Nazareth! Can anything good come from there?" (v. 46 NIV).

John the Baptist began to wonder as well if Jesus might not be all he'd thought. Remember, John the Baptist was pretty amazing. John the Baptist was prophesied to prepare the way for Jesus. And he *did* prepare the way. John the Baptist baptized Jesus. And also remember, after John baptized the Messiah, he heard the voice of God proclaim from the heavens, "This is my beloved Son, with whom I am well pleased" (Matt. 3:17). But John was still a fallen human in a fallen world, susceptible to the same doubts and struggles you and I are. And life was still hard. And John ended up in prison.

It should not shock us that even after all he'd seen and even after clearing the way for Jesus, John could be in that low situation, considering this Jesus and wondering if maybe he had the wrong guy. *You're the guy?* Like, *Where's the white horse? Where is the gravitas of presence? Why am I here in prison right now?*

John, the Baptizer of Jesus. John, the prophesied camel-hair-clad forerunner of the Messiah. John, who heard the voice of God, said, "Jesus, are You really the one? Is this real? Because it doesn't seem to be working."

How did Jesus respond? He responded as the God of all mercy.

> Jesus replied to them, "Go and report to John what you hear and see: The blind receive their sight, the lame walk, those with leprosy are cleansed, the deaf hear, the dead are raised, and the poor are told the good news, and blessed is the one who isn't offended by me." (Matt. 11:4–6)

Jesus built up John's faith. Jesus said, "It's real, John. The blind are seeing just like the prophets said would happen. The lame are walking, just as was foretold. The dead are raised, John. The good news is being proclaimed. I'm exactly who I'm supposed to be."

So that's the start of Matthew 11. John says, . . . *You*? Jesus, says, *Yes*.

But then we see, at the end of the chapter, Jesus offering not just faith but rest. Rest for the weary.

> "Come to me, all of you who are weary and burdened, and I will give you rest. Take my yoke upon you and learn from me, because I am lowly and humble in heart, and you will find rest for your souls. For my yoke is easy and my burden is light." (Matt. 11:28–30)

I often feel burdened. I am so often weary. I live in twenty-first-century America, where there are physical comforts galore that the disciples could have only dreamed of. The people who were alive when Jesus was here experienced weariness and doubt and discouragement, but with no air conditioning. They had no Zoloft prescriptions and limited access to queso. I don't want to be silly, but can you imagine? We take for granted how many temporary comforts we have access to in our weariness. The people of Jesus's time could have related to us on many levels, but they had very few physical comforts to throw at their weariness. And perhaps that was for the best. Maybe ruling out the endless buffet of false comforts means we get more quickly to the real thing.

Humble Jesus came for the weary. Lowly Jesus said, "I will give you rest."

Here in the 2020s, we can take a sleeping pill if we need an extra restful night. We can binge-watch a show or play a phone game if we want to forget our burdens for a little while. But we know, underneath all the streaming and clicking that those modern helps don't really do it for us, do they? We remain weary. Days drag on and pain stacks up and we want a soul-deep rest that can't be found anywhere in this world.

But humble Jesus came and spoke truth to the doubters and shed blood for the sinners so we can look ahead with restful souls to the victorious Jesus of Revelation 19. Humble Jesus will still be the One with fire in His eyes and lightning in His fist. Lowly Jesus can give us strength and relief and rest because He is also the One who will one day conquer everything that ruins rest. I mean, He told John He could raise the dead. Why wouldn't we believe He can raise the weary?

A Future Brighter Than Retirement

My oldest daughter, the retirement home lover, is growing up and processing adult stresses and the weight of worldly responsibilities. She often says, "I don't want to grow up. It looks hard."

And every once in a while, we whisk her away to a land where people move slowly and have helpers who serve them with pre-planned activities and few expectations. Man, that does sound pretty great, doesn't it?

Now, she's too young to grasp what it must be like to live in constant arthritic pain, what it might be like to battle the change of pace and loneliness that can come with assisted living. She doesn't know what it's like to have lived so long that most of what you spent your life building is gone. From my young teen's vantage point, old age is just all bells and whistles and bingo nights.

What my little girl is truly longing for is the absence of stress and fear and pain and planning. She is longing to be taken care of.

Aren't you?

If so, consider Isaiah 46:4. God was talking to the Israelite people, but we, His covenant people who live today, can be sure that our Creator loves us and promises to care for us the same way:

> "I will be the same until your old age, and I will bear you up when you turn gray. I have made you, and I will carry you; I will bear and rescue you."

How beautiful. That's better than a retirement home. Our God, who made us, who died for us, who rose from the grave for us, does not take breaks, does not take paychecks, and does not change. But He does carry. He can bear us up. He's an always able Rescuer and Sustainer when we're weary.

What a stunning contrast to the first verse in Isaiah 46.

> Bel bows down, Nebo stoops low; their idols are borne by beasts of burden. The images

> that are carried about are burdensome, a burden for the weary. (v. 1 NIV)

Bel and Nebo are the names of the false gods of Babylon. And Bel and Nebo have to be carried around by animals. Bel and Nebo are gods that are also burdens out of necessity. They are made of heavy, earth-sourced materials—not to mention they are just statues and therefore not alive—which means they can't carry themselves, much less those who weary themselves in their service. Bel and Nebo are frauds; they are carried about. Bel and Nebo tire out their followers. Even the beasts that carry them get tired of their weight. But instead of requiring us to carry Him around, the One True God says the opposite: "I will be the same until your old age, and *I* will bear *you* up when you turn gray. I have made you, and *I* will carry *you*; I will bear and rescue *you*."

And not only does our unchanging Father watch over us, carry us, bear us up in our old age, but remember where He will ultimately carry us:

> "Don't let your heart be troubled. Believe in God; believe also in me. In my Father's house are many rooms. If it were not so, would I have told you that I am going to prepare a place for you? If I go away and prepare a place for you, I will come again and take you to myself, so that where I am you may be also. You know the way to where I am going." (John 14:1–4)

It gives me chills. We are going Home. Through Christ, we get the comfort of a real home, a forever home, a home with many rooms, with perfect comfort, perfect peace, and the perfect love of our perfect Father. I'll try to convince my daughter that there will also be pre-planned activities.

Living Hopeful-ish with the Apostle Peter

Prior to pregnancy, and with writing this book in mind, I started a little web series called "Living Hopeful-ish with Scarlet Hiltibidal." Until I surrendered my year to throwing up daily and moaning "Get this baby out of me" incessantly, I committed to posting weekly episodes, where I'd share some Scripture and talk through articles I'd written about pursuing a life of hope in a world that often looks hopeless.

I had my daughters make me a bedazzled poster board sign that is still taunting me, push-pinned on the white wall in my bedroom, a daily reminder of the weekly commitment I haven't even attempted to keep for almost nine months now. But what I had in mind before laying down for forty weeks was to help others, and myself, live a 1 Peter life.

Remember what you read in chapter 1:

> Blessed be the God and Father of our Lord Jesus Christ. Because of his great mercy he has given us new birth into a living hope through the resurrection of Jesus Christ from the dead and into an inheritance that is imperishable,

> undefiled and unfading, kept in heaven for you. (vv. 3–4)

If you haven't done it lately, I recommend you read through 1 Peter in its entirety. It won't take you long. It's only five chapters. But, for the sake of time and book space, I'll just skip to the very end, that I mentioned earlier, where Peter reminds us what God will do, after we have "suffered a little while."

In 1 Peter 5 verses 6 through 9, Peter reminds us to humble ourselves before God, and that we can release our cares to Him, because He cares about us. Then, he warns us to be sober-minded and alert against the devil, and then we arrive at beautiful verse 10: "The God of all grace, who called you to his eternal glory in Christ, will himself restore, establish, strengthen, and support you after you have suffered a little while."

There are some more benefits right there. God will restore, establish, strengthen, and support us. Don't gloss over those words. They are so incredible.

He will restore. The word *restore* means "to bring back, to reinstate." Are you reading this book and feeling like I've been feeling because of how much you've lost? I've lost people. I've lost health. I've felt close to losing hope, at times. But, God promises, He will restore what's been lost. That's a beautiful promise.

He will establish. To *establish* is "to set up on a permanent basis." If I had to succinctly explain the pain of the past few years, I'd say my family has suffered the loss of a life we felt was established. Our church felt secure. Our friendships felt secure. Our jobs felt secure. The health and presence of my loved ones felt secure. But life will show you nothing is secure. Nothing on this fallen earth is permanent, apart from God and His people. But when we look toward our brilliant future, we see that God promises to establish us. We will, one day, live in a perfect, Eden-esque world again where we are permanently secure and nothing can be lost.

He will strengthen. *Strengthen* means "to make or become stronger." This whole section we're in is about the weariness we feel when life beats us up. Loss and disappointment make us feel physically, mentally, emotionally, and spiritually weak, right? It's tempting to be like a granny in a nursing home, sitting in the dark, forgetting the benefits. But we don't have to live that way. We weren't meant to live that way. We were created to enjoy God. We were created to walk in the light with other believers, even when (maybe *especially when*) we're not feeling our brightest or shiniest. Remember God's promises and remember that He uses His people to encourage and comfort and strengthen the saints. He will strengthen you. Don't hide from Him or from your community.

And the last thing we see in that verse is that He will support us. *Support* is "to bear the weight of, to hold up." Right here, at the end of 1 Peter, we're reminded that eternity doesn't rise and fall on our strength, or our work, or our efforts. We can lean on the Lord. He will always be strong enough to support us, to hold us up, to carry the heavy things we can't, and He will never need for us to take care of Him. If you and your parents get old enough, the roles will reverse. But that will never be so with God. He will always be our caretaker. We will always be His dependent children.

It brings tears to my eyes, walking through these realities. I've read these verses so many times, but there's something about slowing down and thinking about what the words are actually saying that is so powerful.

The benefits of being a child of God are unbelievable. And after we've suffered through the joys and heartbreaks of this life, we'll arrive, some of us bolting through the door, but many of us weary, maybe limping, but right there at our Father's house, where we can collapse in His care and be restored by His love. Forever.

I pray that my daughters see this tangible hope in me. And on the days or the months or the years that hope is harder to come by, I pray that they see me abiding and pursuing and fighting to keep my eyes on what is true.

I pray that the Lord will give us the grace to fix our eyes on this future hope that is so much greater than Granny's sweet pad. We will turn gray, but we will be carried, and we will be carried Home.

Chapter 6

The Power of a Pillow Nest[7]

I need to tell you about my pillow nest. I developed this practice sometime during the Covid shutdown insanity, but I've got to say, years later, it continues. I've pretty much turned my bed into a cocoon of safety, warmth, and happiness.

Here is the formula. You'll need three to five regular pillows of varying softness and firmness, a neck pillow, a fuzzy blanket, an eye mask, iPhone, airpods, and a favorite T-shirt (mine was given to me in a garbage bag of clothes my sister didn't want and it actually was her college ex-boyfriend's shirt. I've yet to find a shirt that's better for pillow nest-ing than a sister's ex-boyfriend's ex-tee).

Okay, here's what you do. Put two pillows into a V-shape and then lay one on top, as a connecting pillow. Place your neck pillow up around your forehead area and lean back. Make sure to be wearing the sister's ex-boyfriend tee and your sleep mask.

When you wake up in the morning, don't get up. Now is the time to incorporate the fuzzy blanket. Wrap it around your head and shoulders like it's a Christmas play costume, where you're playing Mary, mother of Jesus. Now, you can utilize the phone and the airpods as you scroll through funny online videos and/or listen to a podcast while playing a phone matching game such as the classic "Royal Match," as you are lulled back into a peaceful morning slumber.

Sometime in the past couple years, I became obsessed with my pillow nest situation. And it's amazing. Like, really great. And I hope you enjoy your own pillow nesting, but of course I must disclose that it doesn't offer a fully sustainable comfort.

The past couple years, as my family faced its onslaught of sadness, my usual baseline fear and anxiety surged. I don't think I'm alone in feeling like the last few years have made our human fragility glaringly obvious––impossible to ignore, even from the fortress of a pillow nest.

Better Than a Pillow Nest

Months after all my tragedies that felt like *boom-boom-boom*, I still felt like I was looking over my shoulder waiting for the next tragedy to strike. *What's next! Is the world falling apart? Is Jesus coming back today?* And then I came across Psalm 119, not as I was doing a daily Bible-reading plan, but while I was doing my pillow nesting and looking at a social media post at 3:00 a.m.

Someone in my feed, the daughter of a family friend, shared about how she'd just memorized that psalm and it changed her life.

I took a break from social media-ing and looked it up on my phone, and the Holy Spirit pierced my weary, scared soul.

Read these words out loud if you can.

I am weary from grief;
strengthen me through your word.
Keep me from the way of deceit
and graciously give me your instruction.
I have chosen the way of truth;
I have set your ordinances before me.
I cling to your decrees;
Lord, do not put me to shame.
I pursue the way of your commands,
for you broaden my understanding.

Teach me, LORD, the meaning of your
  statutes,
and I will always keep them.
Help me understand your instruction,
and I will obey it
and follow it with all my heart.
Help me stay on the path of your commands,
For I take pleasure in it.
Turn my heart to your decrees
and not to dishonest profit.
Turn my eyes
from looking at what is worthless;
give me life in your ways.
(Ps. 119:28–37)

That's actually just a small part of the longest chapter in the Bible. But, man. It got me.

I've heard many preachers say, "We don't just read the Bible . . . the Bible reads us." But there's nothing like experiencing it for yourself.

God knew I was looking to "worthless things" for comfort. Pillow nests and viral videos and snacks and show-binging and anything that could make me stop dwelling on the pain, grief, and hard questions. I was weary with grief and God strengthened me through His Word. The Spirit lovingly got my attention that night. He reminded me that His Word, His decrees, His commands point me to true Comfort. Jesus is the only One who can "broaden my understanding." Jesus is the only One who can quiet my questions.

Jesus is the One who made us and everyone we love (check out John 1 and Col. 1:16). And He came here, to this broken, sad, weary place to save us and give us hope and peace and power. I do hope you get to experience the fleeting-floaty feeling of being in a pillow nest, but way more than that, I hope you seek and find the only Comfort that is true and powerful and eternal. Open your Bible. Ask the Spirit to read you. Jesus is better than pillows.

Did Jesus Need a Pillow Nest?

To me, the humanity of Christ is one of the most comforting realities of our faith. When we're weary, beat up, dejected, and suffering, we can look at the Gospels and remember the exhaustion experienced by Jesus—the only being who could have opted out of exhaustion, weariness, and need.

When I feel weary and weak and overwhelmed by troubles, I tend to focus more on Christ's deity, His supremacy, His power, His loftiness. And He is all those things. But He also made Himself small for us. He made Himself able to identify with us, able to be weak and tired and grieving.

Let me teach you a theological term about this. My pastor for years in Nashville said that he would never stop teaching theological language to people in the church, because if we can learn to order using fancy coffee words at Starbucks, we can learn to communicate theologically. My go-to order from a few years ago is a great example: grande iced brown sugar oat milk shaken espresso with vanilla sweet cream cold foam.

That was my drink of choice for a while, and if we can learn to order a grande iced brown sugar oat milk shaken espresso with vanilla sweet cream cold foam, then we can learn theological terms to help us better understand and communicate about the God of the Universe.

Hypostatic union is the theological term for the reality that Jesus Christ is 100 percent God and 100 percent human, simultaneously. Said another way, *hypostatic union* means Jesus is fully God and man at the same time. This is a massively important concept that has been a foundational truth of the Christian faith for thousands of years. Without the truth of the hypostatic union, nothing else matters. If Jesus was not fully human, then He could not stand in our place, He could not live in our place, He could not receive the penalty of sin in our place, He could not die in our place, and He could not rise from the dead in our place. After all, *humans* introduced the global problem known as sin. We made the way for it. We opened the door. We created the human condition, as it were. So if humans introduced the problem, then a human had to solve it. Jesus is that human. Put differently, if Jesus came as a ring-tailed lemur, well, He'd maybe have saved the ring-tailed lemurs—but not the humans. For His work to save us from sin, suffering, and death, He had to become like us. If He wasn't human, we'd be in a real bind.

But, of course, if He was *only* human, we'd also be in a bind. He also had to be God. If He wasn't also God, He would not have the power for any of those actions to have meaning or to have supernatural, eternal impact. After all, the problem of sin, suffering, and death eventually spilled over onto the whole world, infecting everything humans were supposed to oversee with care and responsibility. But all those plants and animals under their care? They die just like humans do. It's a bad picture. That's a massive problem—a God-sized problem, you could call it. This means it needs a God-sized solution. No ordinary man could pull it off.

On top of the sheer scope of the problem, there's the power and determination and *sinlessness* it requires to defeat sin and death on our behalf. It's not like some random guy off the street could crawl up on a cross and get the job done. Even if he gave his life as a noble sacrifice, is this person's sacrifice a pure and sinless one, the kind of sacrifice the Lord of the Universe would require? No. That guy off the street would mean well, but he'd be just as guilty of all the same sorts of sins as you and me. That guy off the street is infected with the same human condition as the rest of humanity is. We need someone who isn't. We need someone pure. The person who offers himself as a sacrifice for humanity has to be a perfect, righteous, never-sinning substitute for us. And only God is perfect like that. It means that for the Savior to meet God's standards, he'd have to be God himself. And yet, because of all the reasons listed before, he'd have to be human at the same time. So, as you can see, the hypostatic union matters because it expresses that Jesus was *both. He's exactly what we needed.*

This is what David Mathis, the executive editor of *Desiring God*, writes about this concept:

> Jesus has two complete natures: one fully human and one fully divine. What the doctrine of the hypostatic union teaches is that these two natures are united in one person in the God-man. Jesus is not two persons. He is one person. The hypostatic union is the joining (mysterious though it be) of the divine and the human in the one person of Jesus.[8]

That guy is really smart. My husband prefers to explain it by making a peanut butter and jelly sandwich, which he did recently during a sermon.

He believes the jelly is not as good as peanut butter, so the jelly represents humanity. The jelly represents temporary bodies made in the image of God. The jelly represents human weakness, human frailty, human temptation, brokenness. It represents human joys, happiness, grief, and everything else that makes up the experience of being human. That's the jelly.

The peanut butter represents the divine. The peanut butter represents the fullness of God, the nature of God. The peanut butter represents permanence, perfection, sovereignty, infinite power, infinite wisdom, the understanding of and the authority over everything there is. The peanut butter represents Godness, and the jelly represents humanness.

And the point Brandon makes is that when you put together a peanut butter and jelly sandwich, you don't end up with something that has 50 percent less jellyness than it had before the joining and 50 percent less peanut butterness than it had before the joining. Instead, you end up with something that is 100 percent peanut butter and jelly.

Jelly doesn't become less jelly, and the peanut butter doesn't become less peanut buttery. The jelly is still fully jelly and the peanut butter is still fully peanut butter, and together it's peanut butter and jelly. It is also delicious.

And that is what happened with the eternal son of God in John 1.

> In the beginning was the Word, and the Word was with God, and the Word was God. He was with God in the beginning. Through him all things were made; without him nothing was made that has been made. (vv. 1–3 NIV)

Then, in verse 14 (NIV), "The Word became flesh and made his dwelling among us. We have seen his glory, the glory of the one and only Son, who came from the Father, full of grace and truth."

A human and divine sandwich was made. Jesus was 100 percent God. Jesus was the creator of the world, and then He put on 100 percent flesh and dwelt among us. That's the hypostatic union. That is two natures in one person.

We also see the hypostatic union in Hebrews 1:3 (NIV):

> The Son is the radiance of God's glory and the exact representation of his being, sustaining all things by his powerful word.

Jesus was a human *and* He was the 100 percent exact representation of God, sustaining all things. Then—and this is a heartbreakingly beautiful truth—the God of the universe, the pure and perfect and all-powerful and our minds can't even wrap around Him God, put on a body that was as human as mine and yours. God did that.

> For there is one God and one mediator between God and mankind, the man Christ Jesus, who gave himself as a ransom for all. (1 Tim. 2:5–6)

"The man Jesus Christ." Paul says this man is our mediator. Not was. Jesus didn't just temporarily take our likeness on the cross, but He kept it forever. He is in a glorified human body right now. And Jesus didn't just temporarily care about us on the cross, but He is caring about us right now. He is interceding for us right now. The God-man, 100 percent human and 100 percent divine, is 100 percent for us, forever.

The hypostatic union is infinitely better than a grande iced brown sugar oat milk shaken espresso, and it means that Jesus truly knows your weakness. Jesus was weary. Jesus got thirsty.

> After this, when Jesus knew that everything was now finished that the Scripture might be fulfilled, he said, "I'm thirsty." A jar full of sour wine was sitting there; so they fixed a sponge full of sour wine on a hyssop branch and held it up to his mouth. (John 19:28–29)

"I thirst." Through those two words, we have the opportunity to see that the one true God understands us. Because Jesus is fully human, He can sympathize with our thirst, with our weariness, with our everything.

You see, the whole point of Jesus putting on flesh and dwelling among us, was so He could experience what we experience, feel what we feel, know the pain we know, face the temptations we face, all while handling everything perfectly, as we could not.

Jesus was dying and He was thirsty. Jesus, fully human, knows what it means to experience need, discomfort, and dissatisfaction. He was beaten and tortured for hours, and He needed something to drink. Jesus had a 100 percent human body that could not survive without water. He faced what we face. Jesus can understand your pain, your need, your struggle, your thirst.

The hypostatic union means Jesus knows how we hurt.

A few years ago, I spoke several times at a church deep in the farmland of Missouri, in a community that had lost four people to suicide in the last year. They talked about it so much because people they love had died in a tragic way. And they were hurting. And I could sympathize with them I know how much that hurts.

But you know who sympathizes with those Missourians even more? Jesus. Jesus hurts with them. Jesus understands them. Jesus knows what it is like to be one of us. Jesus lost a close friend to death. The Bible tells us Jesus's friend Lazarus died, and how did Jesus respond to that death? He cried. It's the shortest verse in the Bible. John 11:35. "Jesus wept." When you weep, God Himself understands. Jesus, as God, became fully human to fully suffer the needs and griefs of His people. No other God even claims to be like that.

Our God got thirsty like us. Our God lost loved ones like us. Have you been betrayed by a friend? Jesus knew that pain too. Judas sold out his friend for thirty pieces of silver and a kiss on the cheek. Do you see? Jesus not only became human so He could save you in every way, He also became human so He could *sympathize* with you in every way. The author of Hebrews puts these things side by side:

> For this reason he had to be made like them, fully human in every way, in order that he might become a merciful and faithful high priest in service to God, and that he might make atonement for the sins of the people. Because he himself suffered when he was tempted, he is able to help those who are being tempted. (Heb. 2:17–18 NIV)

And the author of Hebrews doesn't stop there he reiterates the fact that Jesus's humanity is meant to be a comfort to us and remind us that he really does get our life and our struggles, which, in turn, produces in us great hope and boldness:

> For we do not have a high priest who is unable to empathize with our weaknesses, but we have one who has been tempted in every way, just as we are—yet he did not sin. Let us then approach God's throne of grace with confidence, so that we may receive mercy and find grace to help us in our time of need. (Heb. 4:15–16 NIV)

Are you suffering? Are you exhausted? Are you overwhelmed with grief? Are you betrayed? Jesus 100 percent understands you.

In an article titled "Why Jesus's Humanity Matters as Much as His Divinity," Michael J. Kruger writes,

> Jesus could only represent humans if he became a human—a real human. And if he cannot represent us, then he cannot redeem us. Or as the church father Gregory of Nazianzus once said, "That which he has not assumed he has not healed."
>
> Don't miss the incredible implication of this truth: our salvation is as dependent on Jesus's humanity as it is on his divinity. But there's more. It's not just that we need a representative. We need a representative who *sympathizes* with us and *understands* us. We need

> someone who knows what it is like to live in a dark, fallen world.[9]

As the verses above in Hebrews state, *He did just that.* Jesus put on flesh, so He could be in our shoes. He was born as a baby, dependent on caretakers to meet His physical needs. He lived through the helplessness of being a real human child, walked through relationships with broken, mean, messy, cruel people. He lived life in brokenness, like we do. Then, He died the gruesome, torturous, humiliating death we deserved, allowing Himself to be separated from God—the greatest sacrifice.

But don't forget the peanut butter. Because of His deity, we know the rest of the story. We know He didn't stay dead, giving us **hope** that there *is* someone who can actually swoop into what looks hopeless here, to save the day, to save our souls.

We know the end of the story. We know that He is no longer suffering. He is no longer dead. He's alive and sitting on His glorious throne. But for thirty-some years, He was here. He was hurting. He was daily in need of pillow nesting. The most dramatic examples that we typically think of when it comes to the physical hurts of Jesus are His crucifixion, His betrayals, and His temptations in the desert. But we must remember that He lived so many day-to-day moments outside of those extreme instances—moments where He had to suffer ordinary pain and discomfort, just like we do.

Too Cool for Midlife Seminary

Have you ever been in a situation where you feel above what you're experiencing? Luckily, this is just a book. You don't have to admit it to anyone, because what a yucky thing to admit. But you know what I mean. Maybe you're doing something you're overqualified for and the people around you are unaware.

My husband is in his forties, but just now finishing up his master's degree. It's all online. One of his professors the other day gave him an A+ on a paper and left a note that said something like, "Wow! This is great writing. You have a real future ahead of you. Keep honing your communication skills and I'm sure you'll do great things."

The receiver of that message was my silver-fox of a husband who has worked for many years in publishing. The professor didn't know who he was emailing and what career stage the recipient of that email was in. My gray-bearded man, who has had a long career in publishing already, was getting a "Go get 'em, champ!" email, while he sat in his basement. He told me about the grade and the note with a chuckle.

Brandon said, "I had to respond and tell him that I'm actually an old man who worked in publishing for a long time, and most people I know are authors who are way better writers than I am."

The good grade and "encouraging note" from the professor made him feel, for a moment, like writing papers online in his basement was beneath him. We've all had those moments.

On an infinitely more intense scale, Jesus left the perfect comfort and glory of the heavenly home and downgraded to a body that hurts, amongst a people that doubt and jeer and mock. He didn't get A+ papers with notes that said, "Good job being King of the Jews." He got mocked for claiming to be the King He was. He received rejections and betrayals and all forms of evil from the people He'd come to save.

Jesus was in need of a pillow nest more than any of us can even fathom. And He went to the Father. Just like we can.

Remember in chapter 1 of this book, when we looked at Jesus sweating blood before His crucifixion?

In Luke 22, you can read about Jesus's prayer in the garden of Gethsemane. Jesus talked to and submitted to His Father and said, "Father, if you are willing, take this cup away from me—nevertheless, not my will, but yours, be done" (v. 42).

Immediately, we see that God responded. He didn't take the cup of impending and actual doom away from Jesus. But He comforted His Son in the midst of the pain: "Then an angel from heaven appeared to him, strengthening him" (v. 43).

Jesus didn't try to distract Himself from what was coming. He didn't look for comfort in any earthly way. Instead, He took His troubles to His Father and received the comfort and strengthening of an angel. Hebrews 5:7 (NIV) sums up His approach this way: "During the days of Jesus' life on earth, he offered up prayers and petitions with fervent cries and tears to the one who could save him from death, and he was heard because of his reverent submission." Do you hear that? Prayers. Petitions. Fervent cries. Tears. How human is that?

In other words, when Jesus faced the hard and the sad and the wearying—even death—He ran *each and every time* to the One who understood Him. He did exactly what the Scriptures tell us to do: He approached God's throne of grace with confidence, so that He might receive mercy and find grace to help Him in His time of need. And in turn, after He finished His work and "became the source of eternal salvation for all who obey him," He was then "designated by God to be [our] high priest" (Heb. 5:9–10 NIV)—to be the One who understands us down to the cellular level, and can mediate for us whenever we need Him to.

Run to Him, if you're weary. He knows what it's like because He's human. And He can be trusted with the power to get through it because He's God.

Chapter 7

Pillow Nest Part 2: When the Cancer Comes Back

The day I went to my first book meeting, my mom came over to babysit my kids. I think she was wearing a head covering, because she was right in the middle of her cancer treatment, but she still wanted to babysit as often as possible.

She had just been diagnosed with stage three metastatic breast cancer. She had the big surgery and the chemo and the radiation. All of it. And though she was smack-dab in it, she still wanted to be there for me. I remember what I was wearing that day because she brought me outside by the pretty tree to take pictures of me headed to my big book lunch. I was smiling overly big, and so was she. Baby on her hip, bald, and taking pictures of my dream coming true.

It was a wild year for her, and for us, watching her go through it. But I always tell people how instructive and moving it was, watching my mom walk through something that looked so hopeless, as a follower of Jesus.

Every time I travel and speak, one of the stories I end with is talking about the first time I visited my mom at the infusion clinic during chemo. She was in the last room at the end of a long, white hallway and I remember all I could think was a quote from Psalm 23. *This is "the valley of the shadow of death,"* I thought, as I passed woman after woman with sad, pained, tired, and hopeless faces. But then there was my mom at the end of the hallway, curly lavender wig, Venti Frappuccino, laptop open and big Bible on her lap, showing me what it looks like for a believer to walk through it.

Well, just this month, she had a bronchoscopy that revealed a concerning lymph node that has been making it hard for her to breathe and giving her a horrible cough that has lasted a year. It's been nine years since she fought cancer, since her hair grew back, since she returned to being her vibrant, wacky self.

But, what now? What do you do when the cancer comes back?

She woke up from this last procedure to her previously hopeful surgeon saying that he was "concerned."

I texted her that night and asked if she was worried, and she texted back, "Good question. I'm envisioning the different scenarios and how Jesus would act in each situation. He did ask God to 'let this cup pass from me,' but 'thy will be done.' He wouldn't have a nervous breakdown or commit suicide or drive into a tree purposely. Or overdose on purpose. Or lay in bed all day. At the risk of looking like an aging actress who's using this to get attention, I think [documenting] it with Scripture might be a good testimony . . ."

Nine years later, I'm about to be in the diaper phase again. I still attend exciting book meetings. And my mom's envisioning her possible departure from this life, and wondering what it looks like to handle it like Jesus.

After church last week, my family met up at our favorite Mexican place, and my mom told Brandon that if her cancer was back, like she suspected, she just wanted to go to Paris, play with her grandbabies, and then "sloop" up to Jesus.

She made some jokes about dying, we joined her vibe, and I went home and cried.

Since that lunch, her breathing rapidly got worse, her biopsy results came back, and we all got the news we hoped we wouldn't. The lymph node had a cancerous tumor in it, and it was (is) blocking her windpipe. A few days after that news, we learned that the tumor was inoperable, and the doctor said her cancer was likely too widespread to get rid of. There would be no chemo and she'd get as many stay-comfortable meds as she wanted.

Not good news.

I know she must be scared sometimes. I know she's not always joking and strong, but I also know that her testimony is true. I know she believes that she'll be with Jesus either soon or really soon.

Oh, that I could follow that example. That I could look at things as bleak as even death and say, with confidence, "The Lord is my shepherd, I have what I need" (Ps. 23:1).

I don't want my mom to die. I don't want my children to lose their Bam Bam. I can't not cry when I think about Baby James never knowing her.

But I believe in Jesus, so I believe in heaven. I believe in His no-more-tears promises, so I can grieve, and pre-grieve like someone with hope. My hope might not feel strong. Right now, there might be an emphasis on the "ish" in hopeful-ish. But I'm not hoping in the strength of my hope. I'm hoping in the God who made my mom. The God who gave her the gifts she has. The God who poured love into her, that spilled out onto me for the last thirty-eight years. I have hope in the God who will fully heal and restore every broken part of her. I have hope that when I see her again, she will be whole in every way.

Jesus entered into hopelessness and experienced the turmoil of this world, so that we wouldn't have to face terminal cancers and broken relationships alone. He suffered, so that He could save. He gave up all comfort, so that He could become our Pillow Nest. He is my mom's Pillow Nest, as she goes from this broken life to the perfect one awaiting her.

> The LORD is my shepherd;
> I have what I need.
> He lets me lie down in green pastures;
> he leads me beside quiet waters.
> He renews my life;
> he leads me along the right paths
> for his name's sake.
> Even when I go through the darkest valley,
> I fear no danger,
> for you are with me;
> your rod and your staff—they comfort me.
> You prepare a table before me
> in the presence of my enemies;
> you anoint my head with oil;
> my cup overflows.

Only goodness and faithful love will pursue
me
all the days of my life,
and I will dwell in the house of the LORD
as long as I live. (Ps. 23)

A Pregnancy Pillow Nest from My Mom

The girls and I have been trying to see my parents more often, in this season. Our life is busy, but because of my mom's cancer, we're reminded how short it is too. So that means working more Bam Bam visits into our days than we have in the past. A week or two ago, we were over at her house. She was sitting still in a leather chair drinking hot tea, because every time she got up to move, it would trigger a big coughing jag. Maybe this doesn't sound like a weird thing for a mom to do, to you—sitting in a chair and drinking hot tea—but you have to understand, this is a *very* weird thing for *my mom* to do. She doesn't sit still. Like, I barely remember her ever sitting still in any memory I can pull up. My mom's a mover. She's a shaker. She's a shaker-upper. Hot tea takes too long, when you've got screen plays to write into existence and auditions to run to and an Eiffel Tower to handstand in front of.

She sat in that chair with her tea and listened intently as my girls took turns performing their school things. My youngest is going for "Memory Master" this year at her homeschool-hybrid program and one of the things she has to do is memorize a fourteen-minute song laying out the history of the world from creation until 9/11.

There was no multitasking during this presentation. My mom just sat and listened and smiled and clapped.

The tears we'd entered with were gone by the time we walked to the car, because my mom used her words and time and energy that day to love us, to be hopeful in front of us, to remind us that death is not the end. When we got to the car, my oldest said, "I felt really sad when we first got to Bam Bam's house, but the way she was acting and the things she said made me feel like everything's going to be okay."

And then, right before I pulled out of her driveway, my mom said, "Wait, wait," through coughs, "I have a brand-new body pillow, tags still on, that we're not using that would be perfect for your pregnancy."

"Oh, please no, Mommy," I said, with my car window rolled down, "I have my pillow nest system. It's really good, I promise."

My mom insisted I take it and try it, so I watched her go back inside and return with a giant body pillow. My sick mom, who would be *completely* justified in having her own health and comfort in the front of her mind, was more concerned about mine. She returned, coughing a ton from the walk, with the new pillow nest.

What a beautiful, real-life example of what she's also doing for me and my family spiritually right now. She is not physically comfortable in any way. She is not healthy. She is not strong. She is weary. She is standing at the edge of her life, looking death in the face. But the amazing thing is, she has an overflow of comfort to share. Even sick, even coughing and struggling to breathe, weary to the max, she offers her very own softness and comfort to me, her pregnant daughter. Really, to the whole of our family. Even in her suffering, she is soothing. Consoling. A safe place to land. How? How is she doing that? There is no earthly explanation. It's just Jesus.

> Blessed be the God and Father of our Lord Jesus Christ, the Father of mercies and the God of all comfort. He comforts us in all our affliction, so that we may be able to comfort those who are in any kind of affliction, through the comfort we ourselves receive from God. For just as the sufferings of Christ overflow to us, so also through Christ our comfort overflows. If we are afflicted, it is for your comfort and salvation. If we are comforted, it is for your comfort, which produces in you patient endurance of the same sufferings that we suffer. And our hope for you is firm, because we know that as you share in the sufferings, so you will also share in the comfort. (2 Cor. 1:3–7)

I don't know what you're facing. It may be something even worse than what we've endured as a family lately. And it may come with so much grief you can barely breathe. What I do know after witnessing my mom is this: Even gasping for breath, *hope is possible.* And not just a little bit of it. Not just enough to get you through the day. But enough of it that its level of richness and depth miraculously overflows to those around you. I'm still learning what this looks like in my own life, and I wish I could say I've arrived at embodying it perfectly. But the life of my mom makes it crystal clear: Suffering doesn't mean you have to harden yourself, constantly bracing for impact or protecting yourself from pain. You can stay as soft as a pillow. And, whether cough jagging or not, you can give that softness away.

Chapter 8

Middle-Aged Heartache and Blue Ribbons to Come

My daughters are, um, diverse, when it comes to physical activity. There's the oldest, who gives everything her all—volunteering before she even knows what she's volunteering for, raising her hand to answer before she knows what the question is. Then, there's the youngest, who is naturally athletic and coordinated and loves being physical. And then there is my little indoorsman—sweet Joy. Joy likes to be inside, working with her hands in a climate-controlled environment. All this to say, I had my predictions about how their first "field day" would go.

I didn't see much of my oldest. She was busy. Occasionally, she'd zoom up to show me a new blue ribbon she'd secured. My indoorsman gave full effort, but clearly wasn't having her favorite day. And my youngest, after a few events, covered in sweat and red-faced, started to crumble. See, there were some events where if you won, you got to go to the ribbon table right away and claim your prize, but for most events, volunteer moms stood with clipboards, recording times to then be compared with the hundreds of other little kids at the end.

Though it turned out she was crushing it, my littlest wasn't yet sure she was crushing it. Hours in, she cried, "I never want to come to field day again."

When award time rolled around, she roared back to life while hearing her name and receiving a ribbon. Then again, her name, and a ribbon. Then again. And again. She won or placed in almost every event she participated in.

"Well, do you still never want to come to field day again?" I smiled.

She smiled back, "I love field day."

Thankfully, even our indoorsman secured a ribbon, so we went home a happy, sweaty, victorious bunch.

It makes me laugh, thinking about what a perfect biblical illustration our Hiltibidal field day turned out to be. The apostle Paul, when writing to the church in Corinth, said,

> Don't you know that the runners in a stadium all race, but only one receives the prize? Run in such a way to win the prize. Now everyone who competes exercises self-control in everything. They do it to receive a perishable crown, but we an imperishable crown. So I do not run like one who runs aimlessly or box like one beating the air. Instead, I discipline my body and bring it under strict control, so that after preaching to others, I myself will not be disqualified. (1 Cor. 9:24–27)

Isn't it true that so often in life we feel like our blue ribbon might never come?

Here in my middle-age, the heartaches and heartbreaks of life have stacked up. Sometimes, the prize—the wholeness I'll experience when I'm resurrected and communing with God for all eternity—feels far away. I lose sight of the prize. Here, sweat-covered, red-faced, with the sun beating down, I feel like I'm waiting on a ribbon I might not get. It's hot out here, you know?

But when I feel like that, I'm just like my little one—so caught up in the pain of right now, I lose sight of what's to come. And what's to come, for those of us who follow Christ, is more than a ribbon that you can wear to a field day Olive Garden celebration. The prize is peace. Wholeness. Resurrection life. Reward and renewal and love up close. Forever. What a beautiful promise.

In another letter from Paul, this time to the church in Philippi, he wrote,

> More than that, I also consider everything to be a loss in view of the surpassing value of knowing Christ Jesus my Lord. . . . My goal is to know him and the power of his resurrection and the fellowship of his sufferings, being conformed to his death, assuming that I will somehow reach the resurrection from among the dead. . . . Brothers and sisters, I do not consider myself to have taken hold of it. But one thing I do: Forgetting what is behind and reaching forward to what is ahead, I pursue as

> my goal the prize promised by God's heavenly
> call in Christ Jesus. (Phil. 3:8, 10–11, 13–14)

No matter how difficult life gets here in this broken world, we get to walk through it with Jesus—God made flesh. As we've seen, He understands how hard it is to be human. And He promises us a beautiful future. We've already won the ribbon; we're simply waiting to hear our name called out. The reward is ours, secured, earned by Jesus on our behalf, provided "we suffer with him so that we may also be glorified with him" (Rom. 8:17).

Like a Tornado in the Night

The thing about the Christian life is, in order to enjoy the benefits of walking with God in the right-now, you need to be an active participant in the relationship. In order to reap the benefits of friendship and closeness with God while awaiting the ribbon, you need to spend time learning His voice. When we seek Him with regularity, it prepares us for what's ahead.

My first semester in college, I spent weeks and weeks toting my roommates to and from my parents' house for what the Florida Department of Health called "one of the most active, destructive, and costly hurricane seasons of the past century." School was only an hour from where I grew up in South Florida, so we kept retreating there to avoid incoming storms. In just six weeks, we had five hurricanes that hit land—Bonnie, Charley, Frances, Ivan, and Jeanne.

Now I'm a Middle Tennessean, which means I am more accustomed to tornadoes. Tornadoes don't get names. And there's no warning that allows for college students to flee them. Maybe you get a few hours of warning that conditions are right for a tornado, but when it's actually happening, it's a sprint-to-your-basement type of deal. Prep time, at that point, is minutes, sometimes seconds, so you hope that you have what's important to you in the safest possible place.

Last week, we had one of our closest calls. The sirens went off, I yelled for my children, grabbed our pets, and ran downstairs to shelter in the basement while an EF-3 devastated our neighbors, just 2.1 miles away.

My girls were scared, and we adults were rattled. We were so close to the destruction that we've had to pass right through it several times this week just to get in and out of our neighborhood. We saw the flattened pile of rubble that was the home of a single woman who passed away in the storm. We drove by trees that looked like they'd been bombed and exploded. And we saw dazed neighbors standing by their houses with no roofs or missing second floors.

Tragic. Bizarre. Sobering.

As a Floridian, I grew casual about hurricanes because I experienced so many and came out unscathed. And I've noticed that same attitude developing in me toward tornadoes, as a Tennessean. But driving through the aftermath of a tornado this week, I've been thinking about how we can do the same thing in our faith, which is even more sobering and dangerous than ignoring the warnings of an incoming storm.

What God's Word Says About Readiness

> Don't work only while being watched, as people-pleasers, but work wholeheartedly, fearing the Lord. Whatever you do, do it from the heart, as something done for the Lord and not for people, knowing that you will receive the reward of an inheritance from the Lord. You serve the Lord Christ. (Col. 3:22b–24)

Waiting for the arrival of a powerful storm is a pretty incredible reminder that one day the most powerful Being in the universe is going to arrive, unexpected and without warning, to gather His children and judge His enemies. As much as we can easily get lost in the grocery shopping, career-advancing, and child-raising of this life, that is a true thing that is going to happen. With no indication from The Weather Channel, the King of Everything will appear in the clouds and it will be both a glorious and shell-shocking cataclysm.

That is a moment worth keeping in our minds. But don't take my word for it. Look to Jesus's words on the matter:

> "Therefore be alert, since you don't know what day your Lord is coming. But know this: If the homeowner had known what time the thief was coming, he would have stayed alert and not let his house be broken into. This is why you are also to be ready, because the

> Son of Man is coming at an hour you do not expect." (Matt. 24:42–44)

I used to read these commands about life and Christ's return, and fear I'd be condemned for not being prepared enough. It wasn't until I'd studied Scripture more fully and experienced the mercies of God in my life, that I realized these commands from God are for our protection and flourishing, not for our punishment.

Here's an example of what I mean.

This year, for my family, has been the year of Baby James preparation, and that's meant lots of conversations and planning and preparation and role-playing with my other kids. We've spent time teaching them about the soft spot at the top of Baby Brother's head, and how, if they hold him, they'll need to be sure to support his neck. We've helped my youngest daughter practice, ahead of time, with a baby doll, and warned her about how bad it could be if she's not careful around him when he's born.

"Don't play box ball or flail your arms practicing for tap dancing class when you're near your baby brother," isn't a command or instruction we're giving to kill the good vibes or make our kids fear punishment. We're preparing them and ultimately protecting them and their new brother. We share these instructions because we love their brother and we love them.

In the same way, our heavenly Father's commands are rooted in love, not punishment.

When I had this realization, it helped me consume Scripture, awaiting that day with gratitude rather than panic. I've been able to see Scripture working in my life . . . motivating me to walk in the obedience that leads to my own joy. When we live like that, the Spirit works in us to prepare us for Christ's second coming.

> "My sheep hear my voice, I know them, and they follow me. I give them eternal life, and they will never perish. No one will snatch them out of my hand." (John 10:27–28)

When the sky finally opens and shows us our King, we will hear His voice and follow Him. That's what we prepare for. In the meantime, as we walk with Jesus in the everyday, we learn His voice, follow His leading, and hope to be with Him face-to-face.

We prepare for His coming like we might prepare for a storm or prepare for a field day competition.

Next time I stock up on tornado shelter water bottles, or the next time our family huddles in the storm shelter, I'm going to share with my daughters the comfort of God's Word, and remind them of the beautiful truth that it won't always be this way. Jesus is coming. Eternal safety will arrive for those who know Him. I want my family to live remembering that one day, the skies will split and we won't want to hide. We'll want to sing. We won't fear; we will fall down, rejoicing. We won't even know what hit us.

> "And behold, I am coming soon." (Rev. 22:7a ESV)

How Discipline Is the Antidote to Discouragement

But we're not there yet, right? I don't know about you, but the sky over here in Nashville hasn't cracked open yet. So what do we do while we wait on that glorious day that brings along with it a glorious prize? We train for it. Which, as any athlete will tell you, requires discipline.

Sometimes the last thing a weary comfort-craver wants to think about is discipline. But here's what I'm learning. The disciplines of the Christian life are the very things that help us through the physical and emotional realities of discouragement and exhaustion.

How are we to hold onto hope during those seasons when the blue ribbon feels far away and we don't want to do anything in the meantime?

We need to keep doing the things that help us abide even when all we want to do is hide. Reading God's Word, praying, showing up where God's people are gathered—these are the rhythms that often lead to restoration.

Sometimes, in seasons I'm battling for hope, God's Word is something I consume like cold Gatorade in the hands of a little kid who just finished a field day race. But other times, I resist. I'm in pain. I'm tired. You think I want to read right now? You think I want to read something that might be convicting? That might point out sin in my life? The last thing I want when I'm tired is to be challenged.

But that's because I forget about the supernatural comfort contained in the Word of God, and how beautifully accessible it is to us who will actually open it up. We can cling to God's Word when we're weary.

The spiritual disciplines are just you running to the safest place in which to collapse. That's what we want when we're weary, right? A safe place to collapse. The problem is that we run to the wrong things. Netflix isn't a safe place to collapse. Nor is social media or Chipotle or whatever. But God is. Which is why we run to His Word, to prayer, and to His people. Those are safe places to fall apart and receive exactly what you need.

We all run in some way, to somewhere (or someone). And there is such a thing as running your race in vain (Gal. 2:2). How can we say we've genuinely "thrown off everything that hinders and the sin that so easily entangles" and "run with perseverance the race marked out for us, fixing our eyes on Jesus, the pioneer and perfecter of faith" (Heb. 12:1–2 NIV)? How can we avoid the rebuke that, "You were running a good race. Who cut in on you to keep you from obeying the truth?" (Gal. 5:7 NIV). How can we ensure that we'll one day say along with Paul, "I have finished the race, I have kept the faith" (2 Tim. 4:7)?

We use spiritual disciplines to run toward God and not away from Him.

Physical Discipline for a Daughter with Special Needs

My middle daughter, the indoorsman, spent this past summer doing little workout videos. She's the one we adopted, with various special needs and struggles, and when I noticed she wasn't keeping up as her sisters played and that her body was weaker than it should be, I encouraged her to do these kid workout videos so she could enjoy sprout tag in the front yard and rollerblading in the driveway, rather than standing and watching from the window.

She didn't want to do these workouts, but she does want to be healthy, so she said, "Okay, Mom." And I watched her spend her summer strengthening her body, fifteen minutes at a time. It was amazing. Within just a few weeks, she was out-push-up-ing her sisters and keeping up with them when chasing the dog around the house. Putting in the work pays off, whether it's physical or spiritual.

So how do we rest in Jesus when we are weary? It's the spiritual disciplines through which the Spirit of God helps us abide in Jesus. It's these rhythms that help us enjoy Jesus and find peace in Him.

Are you showing up for the things that could help hope break back in? Let's remember in our weariness the things God can use to help our hearts abide again and hope again. I first heard these categories from Brandon who heard them from his mentor who heard them from his mentors who heard them from some dead scholars from somewhere in history. But

Christians have often categorized the spiritual disciplines into three lists: Inward, Outward, and Communal.

First, there are Inward Disciplines: prayer and Bible study.

The Holy Spirit wants to take God's Word and encourage you where you need to be encouraged, and convict you where you need to be convicted. We can rest in Jesus by remaining in His Word.

If you're not going to God's Word regularly, set a time in your day when you will do it. Just like any other discipline, it won't happen if you don't know when it is going to happen. If you say, "I am going to work out," but don't have a time set, you won't do it. If you say, "I am going to read the Scripture," but don't have a time set, you won't. Choose a time, and dwell with God in His Word.

The same goes for prayer. Often, not knowing what to pray will keep me from praying. I forget that praying, put simply, is talking to my living, active God and Friend. My Father, my Rescuer, my Creator. He has proven how for-me He is, to the grave and back, and He wants me to tell Him about my day. He wants me to align my desires with His as I bring Him my praise and my troubles, and echo His Son as my spirit says, "not my will, but yours, be done" (Luke 22:42).

Then there are Outward Disciplines: serving and giving.

These help us rest in Him, because even as we serve and as we give, we are placed in a dependent posture. It's so beautiful that when we serve others, we are put in a position to rely on God, to need the Spirit to work through us. The same thing happens when you give, because you are basically weakening yourself and trusting God to do more with your less. Often, it is the moment of serving or giving that puts us in a posture of listening to the Spirit and relying on Jesus. If you are not finding your rest in the Father as you want to be, give and serve in the church. Sometimes—as counterintuitive as it sounds—our weariness is removed by serving others.

Lastly, there are Communal Disciplines. We can abide through worship and Christian community.

These are disciplines that must be done in community. You are not supposed to live the Christian life alone. The communal disciplines of gathering together for worship and being in Christian community with others helps us rest in Jesus. It will help us return to Hope. You can't rest in Jesus by yourself.

> Let us hold on to the confession of our hope without wavering, since he who promised is faithful. And let us consider one another in order to provoke love and good works, not neglecting to gather together, as some are in the habit of doing, but encouraging each other, and all the more as you see the day approaching. (Heb. 10:23–25)

I didn't see the beauty of suffering in togetherness until my life circumstances forced me into suffering without it.

When you suffer alone, it's so much harder to remember the truth, to remember the hope. And I think seclusion leads us to view people without grace. It leads us to expect something from them that we should be receiving from God, so then we isolate even more.

Viewing People as "Baby Souls"

Something that's helped me, during seasons of conflict in my marriage, is to intentionally view Brandon as what I call a "baby soul."

Sometimes, this man of my youth, this beautiful, bearded love of my life makes me *so mad*. Some of our tense times have been over the stupidest things. But there have been other seasons—as in the three to four years I've been writing about in this book—where circumstances weakened both of us, where both of us were straining to be hopeful gracious people, unlike the seasons when one spouse struggles and the other can kind of carry things along.

And what has helped me get back on his team in times of conflict has been saying something along the lines of, "I love your baby soul."

What I mean by that is, "I love who you are underneath all these negative emotions we're both feeling." What I mean is, "I know who you really are, like really really, underneath everything we're arguing about. Little, newborn baby Brandon soul. I love that guy."

Brandon had a similar epiphany about how to understand me, just months into our marriage. We got in a big fight over a giant harp.

I just read that last sentence and laughed out loud. It makes me chuckle now, just visualizing the whole ordeal. There was a wealthy family at the church we worked at, and they had a giant, beautiful, ornate harp they were getting rid of. Just some spring cleaning in the mansion, I guess. Time to donate a harp. They were wonderful, thoughtful, generous people. They knew Brandon was a musician, so they offered him the harp.

After church, the Sunday they gave us the harp, he had me hold it up while he went to go talk to a few people.

I don't know what snapped in my brain at that moment, but as I stood, trapped in a hallway balancing a harp for what I deemed way too long, I became enraged. I felt abandoned, forgotten, and ridiculous. Like a pathetic cartoon woman, holding a harp up for a man who didn't seem to be in a rush to come back to her. I could hear his laughter wafting over from the sanctuary, and for some reason, it made me feel pathetic and I just stood with the harp and fought back the tears.

I don't remember what our fight looked like that day. But I remember Brandon responding to my sadness and anger with genuine sympathy.

Later, he told me that how I responded to that harp situation reminded him that I was the grown-up version of the little girl who experienced divorce and trauma and loss. When he remembered that I had once felt entirely powerless and alone in my childhood, he said it gave him compassion for my plight: being stuck alone with the harp.

But that's not an easy thing. It's a discipline thing. You have to condition yourself to view the people in your life as baby souls as you abide in community together.

What Weary Hoping Is and Isn't

The first time I heard about Eugene Peterson was when I was in high school. It was 2002, and a new Bible with very "with it" language had just come out. I got a copy for Christmas. Bible verses and stories that used to sound old and convoluted to me suddenly came to life. In my blue leather King James Bible, Romans 8:1–2 said, "There is therefore now no condemnation to them which are in Christ Jesus, who walk not after the flesh, but after the Spirit. For the law of the Spirit of life in Christ Jesus hath made me free from the law of sin and death."

But, in Peterson's version (known as *The Message*), he paraphrases those verses this way:

> With the arrival of Jesus, the Messiah, that fateful dilemma is resolved. Those who enter into Christ's being-here-for-us no longer have to live under a continuous, low-lying black cloud. A new power is in operation. The Spirit of life in Christ, like a strong wind, has magnificently cleared the air, freeing you from a fated lifetime of brutal tyranny at the hands of sin and death.

It was all very helpful to me. Peterson's paraphrase breathed new life into Scripture for the me of 2002.

Years later, I read one of his books, *A Long Obedience in the Same Direction*. I read it during a time when my faith wasn't new. I'd been walking with Jesus for about twenty years, at that point, and was starting to enjoy the spiritual gifts that come from knowing Jesus for a while.

I was starting to see all those Scriptures I had hidden in my heart over the years, no matter the motivations at the time. (Example: I need to get an A on my Bible verse test! Or I just started working at a church as a twenty-something and want my coworkers to take my faith seriously.) Even the Scriptures I'd learned during those less mature, more me-centric years were changing me, comforting me, correcting and instructing me, as an older Christian.

I wrestled with anxiety a lot, and in the middle of the night, when my thoughts and fears were racing, the Lord would give me words of truth from His Bible, words I didn't even remember I knew. He'd give me those words and still my mind and comfort my soul.

So that's where I was at when I read this book. "A long obedience" proved itself a joy, not a drudgery. There are so many great quotes from that book, but I love what Peterson said here about hope.

> Hoping does not mean doing nothing. It is not fatalistic resignation. It means going about our assigned tasks, confident that God will provide the meaning and the conclusions. It is not compelled to work away at keeping up appearances with a bogus spirituality. It is the opposite of desperate and panicky manipulation, of scurrying and worrying. . . . And hoping is not dreaming. It is not spinning

> an illusion or fantasy to protect us from our boredom and our pain. It means a confident, alert expectation that God will do what he said he will do. It is imagination put in the harness of faith. It is a willingness to let God do it his way in his time. It is the opposite of making plans that we demand that God put into effect, telling him both how and when to do it. That is not hoping in God but bullying God.[10]

Viewing my relationship with the Lord not as a series of spiritual highs, but as a long walk with my Father, has helped me value the "field day" that is this life, so to speak. Isn't every last one of us so much like my little Dewy girl? We strive and we sweat and we work, and so often it looks like our efforts are moot. So often, we want to quit and we want to cry and we just want to be comfortable because this life is exhausting! We are weary—body and soul.

But to we weary ones, Jesus extends His arms.

> "Come to me, all of you who are weary and burdened, and I will give you rest." (Matt. 11:28)

In Jesus, we find rest. Not every day is easy. It's a long obedience in the same direction, but . . .

> "Take my yoke upon you and learn from me, because I am lowly and humble in heart, and you will find rest for your souls." (Matt. 11:29)

Dewy rested and rejoiced at the end of her first field day because her efforts paid off. She received the prize of four ribbons and a snow cone. What we hope in, as believers, is so much better than that. And not only do we have a beautiful and restful inheritance to look forward to, but we can rest assured that it is not our hard work or hamster-wheel running that gets us there. It is walking surrendered with our Savior over the course of a lifetime. We walk; He's done the work. We rest; He carries. And somehow still, there is a blue ribbon to come.

Chapter 9

Why Do We Stop Praying in Our Pain?

I wasn't breathing well again. Recently, my sister, Aubrey, and I were discussing some relational, emotional pain that was causing me to experience an anxiety-related shortness of breath that I've dealt with on-and-off throughout my life. When it is happening, it feels like no matter what I do, or how hard I try, I just can't get a full breath. Also, during these seasons of hyperventilating and stress, I find, weirdly frequently, what I assume to be cancerous tumors (they've yet to be cancerous tumors). The maybe-tumors and shallow breaths led me, again, to an urgent care where I was told familiar things like, "I don't feel any tumors" and "Your lungs are fine."

The all-consuming anxiety that often overtakes my mind can manifest itself in my physical body. During times of stress and sadness, I've broken out into full-body hives. I've had months where I felt like I couldn't swallow. But most often it's the breathing thing. It's like my body remembers being sad and disappointed. It remembers things not working out. And so it responds physically with gasps and boils.

Jesus's physical human body responded to mental turmoil too, you know. The Bible says that He sweated blood when He was looking toward the emotional and physical and spiritual torment of allowing Himself to be crucified by the people He came to rescue. The perfect God-man, Jesus, had a human body that responded to stress in a dramatic and physical way.

In Luke 22:44, Jesus is praying in the garden, right before He is about to be betrayed by Judas and taken to the cross, and Luke says, "Being in anguish, he prayed more fervently, and his sweat became like drops of blood falling to the ground."

Scholars aren't sure about whether the record of Jesus's sweat being "like drops of blood" is a metaphor or literal, but the point is, Jesus was experiencing extreme stress and His body was responding. (By the way, sweating blood is an actual medical thing called *hematohidrosis*, so don't say I haven't taught you anything today.)

Jesus suffered extreme mental turmoil, just like we do. His physical body responded to emotional pain, just like ours do. Jesus Himself suffered with the deep sad feelings of this life. You know who else did? SO many other people recorded in Scripture. I think about David and some of his super sad songs and prayers that you can find in the Psalms. In fact, Bible scholars agree that an estimated two-thirds of the Psalms are psalms of lament. I just listened to an old Tim Keller sermon called "Praying Our Tears," and he admitted that at first glance, he wondered why God would include some of David's prayers that are clearly theologically wrong, speaking specifically of Psalm 39.

The Fleeting Nature of Life
For the choir director, for Jeduthun.
A psalm of David.

I said, "I will guard my ways
so that I may not sin with my tongue;
I will guard my mouth with a muzzle
as long as the wicked are in my presence."
I was speechless and quiet;
I kept silent, even from speaking good,
and my pain intensified.
My heart grew hot within me;
as I mused, a fire burned.
I spoke with my tongue:
"LORD, make me aware of my end
and the number of my days
so that I will know how short-lived I am.
In fact, you have made my days just inches
  long,
and my life span is as nothing to you.
Yes, every human being stands as only a
  vapor. *Selah*
Yes, a person goes about like a mere shadow.
Indeed, they rush around in vain,
gathering possessions
without knowing who will get them.

"Now, LORD, what do I wait for?
My hope is in you.
Rescue me from all my transgressions;

do not make me the taunt of fools.
I am speechless; I do not open my mouth
because of what you have done.
Remove your torment from me.
Because of the force of your hand I am
finished.
You discipline a person with punishment for
iniquity,
consuming like a moth what is precious to
him;
yes, every human being is only a vapor. *Selah*

"Hear my prayer, LORD,
and listen to my cry for help;
do not be silent at my tears.
For I am here with you as an alien,
a temporary resident like all my ancestors.
Turn your angry gaze from me
so that I may be cheered up
before I die and am gone."

Of this psalm, Keller said:

> Now here we have a psalm of David, Psalm 39, and he's wrestling, and he's weeping, and at the very end, look how it ends. It ends in absolute theological incorrectness. Let me tell you what he's saying. Look at it, and I'll paraphrase it. He's saying, "Look away from

> me. Turn your face away from me. Depart from me, that I might have a little bit of peace before I die." And that's how he ends his prayer. This is a unit, this is a prayer, this is a prayer of David, and it ends with such overwhelming feelings that he actually tells God to do the very opposite of what he should be saying to God. We're not supposed to pray like this. We're not supposed to feel like this. We're not supposed to be like this. We're not supposed to talk like this. But he does.[11]

Keller goes on to talk about how much that used to bother him, given the Christian belief that the Scriptures are without error. Then, he came across a phrase in a commentary by Derek Kidner that gave Keller comfort:

> The prayer, "Look away from me," makes no more sense than Peter's, "Depart from me," yet God knows when to treat this plea as he does when Peter says it in Luke 5 or when the crowd says it in Matthew 8:34. . . . The very presence of such prayers in the Scripture is a witness to his understanding. He knows how we speak when we are desperate.[12]

God knows that sometimes, in our pain, we ask Him to go away.

When I was talking about breathing problems with Aubrey a few weeks ago, I'm pretty sure she hadn't heard this twenty-plus-year-old sermon or read that who-knows-how-old commentary, but she has the Holy Spirit and has been walking through the pains of life with His Word since her childhood. So talking to her while I was struggling to breathe was another God-nudge . . . reminding me to come before Him with my darker feelings, no matter how "off" I know them to be. No matter how much I might want Him to look away.

I was simply pacing in my basement, venting about how panicked and sad I felt, and Aubrey suggested we pray.

She started us off thanking God for being approachable, even when we don't feel the right feelings. She mentioned that sometimes we are angry and thanked God for being available and compassionate in the midst of those feelings. What a simple and profound thing to pray. It was such a necessary help for my hopelessness. I remember where I was standing, right under the exposed AC basement vent, when I felt the Holy Spirit, like He always does, gently crack through the hardness of heart I tend to build up when I feel too in-pain, too vulnerable, too sad, too upset. God has and does and will comfort us with His Spirit and His Word . . . often through His people.

During that same season of breathing problems and pain, I was also working through a Bible-reading plan with my teenager, who had picked the book of Job.

Each morning, while putting makeup on, I was listening to my Bible app recount Job cursing the day he was born and cursing his friends for accusing him of bringing God's wrath on himself. Job is another Bible book that is filled with so many painful and honest words from flawed, weak people trying to fear and follow a God so much bigger than them and their problems.

I could have taken note of that right then and brought my own pain before the Lord, but instead, I checked off my "Bible reading" box for the day, sprayed on my makeup setting spray, and continued fretting over my troubles and asking myself, *Why do you continue to put eyeliner and mascara on every morning when you end up crying it all off by 10 a.m.?*

Why was my prayer life so silent when my world was screaming with pain? Why is it sometimes so hard to bring my real feelings to our compassionate and powerful God who has already proven to me and Job and all of humanity that He can handle it? More than just handle it, but *went through it* too? Even Jesus, who planned His whole ministry around the task of dying and raising again for us, who knew He was headed for a cross in Jerusalem during His final week on earth, begged God in a weak moment for the mission to be accomplished in some other way (Matt. 26:39). And when He finally got to that cross and willingly submitted Himself to its pain, this same Jesus cried out with a rawness and brazenness that history's theologians would usually consider improper, unsuitable, or even audacious when lobbed against the Father: "My God, my God, *why have you abandoned me?*" (Matt. 27:46, emphasis added).

If David and Jesus can throw those kinds of questions at God in their most agonizing moments, trusting they are received in an understanding way, why am I so afraid to?

Why Stop Praying?

> "Turn your angry gaze from me
> so that I may be cheered up
> before I die and am gone." (Ps. 39:13)

David is not the only one who feels this way. I think one reason I stop praying when my circumstances feel extra painful is because the problems I'm looking at feel bigger and more tangible than God, who rules over the unseen.

Sometimes, I forget about the unseen. I forget about the power. I forget the promises. Maybe I don't fully forget; I know they're there. But they feel so abstract, I almost doubt their existence. Honestly, sometimes I do doubt their existence.

My preacher-husband was recently teaching on Jude verse 22—"Have mercy on those who waver"—and he shared with the congregation that wavering (or "doubt" as other translations put it) looks different in my life than it does his. "Scarlet and I have doubted and wavered together for eighteen years now," he said. "Sometimes, it's her. Sometimes, it's me. Sometimes, it's neither. Our wavering looks different. Scarlet would tell you that she's had seasons in her weakness where she wonders, *Is this really real? Is this true faith true?* And that's not how I waver. So I can remind her, 'Here's why it's true. It's the truest thing in the world.' For me, the truth of faith seems to always make sense. But I waver in ways Scarlet doesn't. When I'm weak, I don't wonder, *Is the faith real?* I wonder, *Does the faith work? God is real. Jesus is true. The gospel is the hope of the world. But will it not work for me? Where is my living hope? Where is my unspeakable joy?"*

Have mercy on those who waver, even when you are the waverer. It isn't wrong to waver, but it doesn't make sense to run away from the gaze of the God who is "rich in mercy" (Eph. 2:4). Whether you find yourself giving God the silent treatment because you're wondering if He's really there or because you're wondering if He will really work on your behalf, go to Him.

"But God, who is rich in mercy, because of his great love that he had for us, made us alive with Christ even though we were dead in trespasses. You are saved by grace!" (Eph. 2:4–5). The same God who loved you when you were dead will love you when you're doubting. That is the God we can go to, but so often we stay stuck in our lament. So often we hide, and we come by that instinct honestly.

What do I mean?

Back in Genesis, you might remember, God created the world. He created humans from the dust, in His image and said everything was good. Everything was at peace. The world was untainted. The people were unbroken. And most importantly they had what we were made for . . . friendship with God. They lived in the presence of God. The God of the universe not only made them, but He revealed Himself to them in personal ways. They were friends. And it is not hyperbole to say that this is exactly why we exist.

The famous Westminster Catechism says, "the chief end of man is to glorify God and enjoy Him forever."[13] We were made to enjoy God. We were made for friendship with God.

And if this is why we were made, this is the only true satisfaction available to us.

But read what happened in Genesis chapter 3.

> Now the serpent was more crafty than any other beast of the field that the LORD God had made.
>
> He said to the woman, "Did God actually say, 'You shall not eat of any tree in the garden'?" And the woman said to the serpent, "We may eat of the fruit of the trees in the garden, but God said, 'You shall not eat of the fruit of the tree that is in the midst of the garden, neither shall you touch it, lest you die.'" But the serpent said to the woman, "You will not surely die. For God knows that when you eat of it your eyes will be opened, and you will be like God, knowing good and evil." So when the woman saw that the tree was good for food, and that it was a delight to the eyes, and that the tree was to be desired to make one wise, she took of its fruit and ate, and she also gave some to her husband who was with her, and he ate it. Then the eyes of both of them were opened, and they knew they were naked. And they sewed fig leaves together and made themselves loincloths.
>
> And they heard the sound of the LORD God walking in the garden in the cool of the

> day, and the man and his wife hid themselves from the presence of the LORD God among the trees of the garden. (Gen. 3:1–8 ESV)

Adam and Eve, the first people, had perfect friendship with God. They enjoyed Him. He enjoyed them. And God was glorified in that relationship. Satan hated God and, therefore, wanted to ruin that relationship. He wanted God to have no glory and the people to have no satisfaction, so he lied and convinced Adam and Eve that God didn't really love them. That God didn't really want what was best for them. He schemed for them to believe that there was more enjoyment for them another way. They bought it, and then they disobeyed God. They sinned and brought brokenness into their world. Read again how that encounter ended, paying attention to the words in italics:

> And they heard the sound of the LORD God walking in the garden in the cool of the day, and the man and his wife *hid themselves from the presence of the LORD* God among the trees of the garden. (v. 8 ESV, emphasis added)

That is one of the saddest verses in the Bible. Adam and Eve fractured the friendship. Everlasting Love Himself was coming to take a walk with them. The God of the universe came to enjoy the evening with them, but they had believed a lie, and when the guilt and shame set in, they ran from God and hid in the trees.

We have been hiding in the trees ever since. We have been hiding from our Friend, in our frailty, for thousands of years.

But Aubrey helped me remember what we were made for. When she started praying as I walked around my basement, it was a reminder that we were made for real, intimate, personal, go-for-a-stroll-in-the-evening friendship with the One True God.

God made us to be His "tell me about your day" friend, but sometimes we choose to stay covered by shame and shadows instead. Sometimes instead of running to our Father, we run into the trees.

Fourteen years ago, I almost died. My first pregnancy was an ectopic pregnancy, meaning the baby was trapped in the wrong place. One morning, I woke up screaming, paralyzed with pain. And although we didn't know it, my organ had ruptured and I was bleeding internally. I was stiff with pain. It was terrifying for my husband and me, and do you know what he wanted for me? He wanted life for me. But of course, he couldn't save my life. He didn't know the problem, much less how to do the surgery to fix it. You know what he did? He carried me to the car and then he carried me into the ER.

He knew he couldn't heal me, but he knew someone who could and he thought, *I'll go there.* That's what the Christian life is like. As strange as it may sound, that is the beautiful path to peace for us. We don't save ourselves. We don't heal ourselves. We don't satisfy ourselves. The best we can do is stumble into the hospital. We trip and fall out of the trees in which we have been hiding and beg our hearts to remember the One who can heal and save and satisfy. We remember we are safe in Jesus. We are perfect in Him. We are loved to the death. We have a Friend who made worlds for us to enjoy Him.

The first thing our pain should do is push us toward God, not away. We should work, we should run, only to get to Him. In our hurt, our work is to remember He is working. Our striving is to rest in His striving. Our running is really only a running to remember. When your eyes open in the morning, get out of the trees and sprint to the truth. Open the Bible and see: "Oh enemy, it is finished. Oh world, you are overcome. O body of death, praise be to God that Jesus is enough." And every day we can find ourselves in the presence of the Friend for whom we were made. At His right hand are pleasures forevermore. We did nothing to earn them. We do nothing to keep them. We simply help our hearts, and one another's hearts, to remember and rest in the reality that we have what we need in Him. Our God who calls us friends

God is so much bigger and stronger and more powerful and more personal than the things that make me short of breath. He's even bigger than pains so massive they don't compute, such as sudden death. When we get fixated on our pain, we forget God's greatness and nearness and need a tangible reminder, a jolt, a word from God or someone in the spiritual family to help us remember what is true. We can't always remember, on our own, that God is big and loving and true, but we can go to Him. We can. We should. He wants us to follow what we already saw Jesus doing in Luke 22: "being in anguish, *he prayed more fervently*" (v. 44, emphasis added). In the agonies and valleys and shadows, He wants us to share our hurts, not hide our hearts.

> Cast your burden on the LORD,
> and he will sustain you;
> he will never allow the righteous to be
> shaken. (Ps. 55:22)

Section 3

Hope Is for Today and Forever

Now may the God of hope fill you with all joy and peace as you believe so that you may overflow with hope by the power of the Holy Spirit.

ROMANS 15:13

Chapter 10

Holding On to Hope with "Oh Piffle" Peace

"Oh PIFFLE!" That's the phrase Grandma Marlene often said with a smirk when she thought you were being a baby about something. I loved it, and always thought she invented it, like many other words and phrases that were clearly Marlene-originals. But I looked up the word *piffle* the other day, and it turns out, it actually is a real word and it means "nonsense."

Her ability to say "oh piffle" to the things that scared me could be attributed to her Norwegian Viking blood or the fact that she grew up during the Great Depression.

When I was little, she babysat me at her house in Miami Shores and I loved every minute, except when I had to go to the bathroom. The good parts of her bathroom were that: (a) She always had rubber ducks lining the bathtub and (b) She had not one, but two scales. One that was like the one at the doctor's office where you had to move the little thing back and forth, and a digital one.

But the negative was that she allowed a certain spider—a Daddy Long Legs—to live in the corner of the bathroom, near the toilet paper holder.

"A spider? Oh piffle! I love them and keep them around. They eat the mosquitos, you know!"

Piffle could be used in a variety of Grandma-related circumstances. Not just spiders.

"Oh piffle, it's just a thunderstorm, Scarlet!"

"It's just a little shot. Oh piffle, it will be over before it starts."

Sometimes, she'd use her toes to pinch me or my little sister. I'd yelp.

"That was just a love touch, Scarlet! Oh piffle . . ."

Piffle was such a frequent Grandma-ism, that my little sister got an "Oh piffle" tattoo after Grandma died.

Grandma piffled about things large and small, but I knew her long enough and closely enough to know where her strength came from.

Nothing ever seemed to rattle her and just knowing she was existing in the same broken, sad, scary world I lived in always comforted me. Like, *Grandma isn't afraid of this, so maybe I don't have to be either.*

But then, she died. She left where I am. I can't call her. I can't talk to her. I can't ask her to pray for me so I can borrow some of her piffle-infused bravery. Our fearless matriarch just disappeared in a Tennessee hospital.

It's been three years and I'm still heartbroken and I'm still grieving. I told my sister how often I cry about her recently, and Aubrey started laughing and pointed at a giant blown-up photo I stole from my mom's garage of me and Grandma in front of the ice-skating rink at Rockefeller Plaza in New York.

"Maybe you cry about Grandma so often because you have a giant poster of her staring at you right by your bed."

When we lose people we love, we grieve. We miss them. We put giant pictures of them up and rehearse memories. But, thank God, we don't have to grieve like those who have no hope.

In 1 Thessalonians 4, the apostle Paul wrote to the church of Thessalonica and talked about the call to sanctification (*sanctification*, meaning, Christians living as set apart and pursuing holiness). And he concluded the chapter by talking about the comfort of Christ's second coming. He spoke of Christ's return to help believers, both then and now, as we await wholeness in this broken world. He wrote so that we could suffer and grieve and endure like people with a happy ending to look forward to.

> We do not want you to be uninformed, brothers and sisters, concerning those who are asleep, so that you will not grieve like the rest, who have no hope. (1 Thess. 4:13)

I didn't realize it when I was a bathroom scale tester in my grandma's house, but her "oh piffle" peace came from her faith in a powerful God. She could say "piffle" because she had a calm assurance that comes from a lifetime of walking with Jesus.

I think we can all benefit from Grandma Marlene's example of faith as we endeavor to live out the call of Jesus in this so-often hope-crushing world. I aspire to live like Grandma Marlene lived in front of me.

In another of Paul's letters, this time to the church in Corinth, he wrote, "Imitate me as I also imitate Christ" (1 Cor. 11:1). That might sound weird at first glance, but I get what he meant. He wasn't saying, "I'm super awesome, so you should try to be like me." Rather, he was saying, "Because of Jesus, I've found hope in this hopeless world. Follow me, as I follow Jesus."

A Testimony of Peace and Joy

Grandma's health hadn't started going yet. She still set her hair in pin curls most nights, but was getting too tired to put her Christmas tree up and down every year, so she just decided to have a "Christmas Room" and leave the tree up for the rest of her life. That's what she did. It was amazing. Every time I brought the girls over, we would go upstairs and find a fully decorated, fully lit, 8-foot Christmas tree, rain or shine, summer or winter—for years.

I don't remember what prompted it, but one day, when most members of my small family happened to be in one place at the same time, we decided to pray together. We held hands in Grandma's cheery home and I will never forget her prayer.

I don't remember all of what she said, but here's what I'll never forget. "Help us to have joy and peace, because that's our testimony."

What a statement. What a prayer. It struck me because, the thing is, that WAS her testimony! She was praying it there by the Christmas Room, and she was living it. I saw it in how she engaged with the mailman and her neighbors. I saw it in how she faithfully served Wednesday night suppers in the basement of her church. I recognized it more recently, looking through the old journals left behind, where she'd write about new friends who didn't yet know the love of Jesus. She'd write out prayers for them and ask Jesus to help her share His love.

She had obviously prayed that prayer before, and I was one of a lucky handful of witnesses that got to observe the powerful peace of God in the life of an old, faithful woman.

As we walk with Jesus and learn who He really is—loving, sovereign, gracious, carrying, returning—we begin to find "Oh piffle" peace impacting our testimony. I can't imagine what that must feel like after finding Him faithful for seventy years, but I know what it looked like in Grandma Marlene and I want that testimony too.

Ducks in a Row

Grandma is wearing a Santa robe, facing the bathroom sink. It's one of my favorite pictures. Also in the picture, one of my daughters, about five at the time, just watches her smiling, while sitting on top of the closed toilet seat. And on the sink are several yellow rubber ducks in a row.

I love it for so many reasons. Grandma was warm and whimsical. We've already covered the Christmas tree room. But she also had a "Doll Room," floor to ceiling, hundreds of dolls she'd collected over the years. There were fun toys in all the non-themed rooms too (including the bathroom), that she'd change around every time I brought my daughters over to visit.

To me and my girls, she was just magic. To the adults in the family who knew her in a different way, they joked about Grandma's need to have "all her ducks in a row." I'm sure she had that side to her, but I never really saw her fight for control or long to have things her way. With my girls and me, she was more concerned about the ducks (and other toys in other rooms) being enjoyed than orderly.

Maybe I don't remember negative things about Grandma because of the unique nature of a grandmother-grandchild-great-grandchild relationship. But I think it's also because I got to watch her walk with Jesus for so many years, and so I got to see God fulfilling His promises in her. Promises like . . .

> I am sure of this, that he who started a good work in you will carry it on to completion until the day of Christ Jesus. (Phil. 1:6)

Maybe Grandma had a need for control and order and "her way" in her younger years, but by the time I knew her, imperfect as she was, that struggle had faded into the background. The qualities I noticed in her were deep peace, unmistakable joy, and contentment. Love.

From my vantage point, she was an old woman who was strikingly marked by hope.

Maybe Jesus changed her over the decades from someone who worried to someone who rested. From needing control to finding contentment. After all, that is what He said He'd do for His children.

You know, it's funny. A few years before she died, I went over to her house with my little sister, and we sat around her little red table, and I gave them both a personality test that was really popular at the time. My grandma didn't know much about working computers, so while we sat and snacked, I read each question to her and marked her answers, kind of surprised by all of them. When it came time to give her the score, I said, "Grandma, I'm sorry, but you did this wrong. You failed the test!"

"I did not!" she said.

Her results showed that fear and worry about the future was a defining characteristic and struggle of hers, and I just couldn't accept that. The person I knew her to be was so opposite from how she scored on this test. But she said she answered honestly, and that made me think. It made me marvel at how the Holy Spirit can take our sinful tendencies and weaknesses and so dramatically overturn them that our old ways of thinking and being are overpowered by the fruit of the Spirit. Isn't that amazing? It's so amazing and it's so biblical.

In Galatians 5, Paul writes about the Spirit versus the flesh in our lives:

> I say, then, walk by the Spirit and you will certainly not carry out the desire of the flesh. For the flesh desires what is against the Spirit, and the Spirit desires what is against the flesh; these are opposed to each other, so that you don't do what you want. But if you are led by the Spirit, you are not under the law. (vv. 16–18)

I was just the granddaughter, you know? I wasn't in Grandma's head. I didn't know much or see much of her personal private struggles. But she certainly spent her life pursuing hope in Jesus, even while her flesh may have tended toward worry and lack of trust.

We're all weak and flawed. But the longer we walk with Jesus, the more we'll look like Jesus to the people around us, in a way that encourages and comforts and instructs them.

The Bible backs me up on this:

> We all, with unveiled faces, are looking as in a mirror at the glory of the Lord and are being transformed into the same image from glory to glory; this is from the Lord who is the Spirit. (2 Cor. 3:18)

What a beautiful reminder as we battle our own sin struggles as parents and spouses and workers and friends. The Holy Spirit (and often those closest to us) might see and point out our flaws, but we are unfinished works. God is constantly changing and comforting and stretching and renewing us. And when we're with Him in heaven, like my Grandma is now, we'll be finally finished. Complete. Fully at peace with how God ordered our ducks. Praise God.

The Special Honor of Hidden Gifts

Grandma Marlene's testimony shined a spotlight for me on Paul's words to the church in Corinth:

> The parts of the body that seem to be weaker are the ones we can't do without. The parts that

> we think are less important we treat with special honor. The private parts aren't shown. But they are treated with special care. The parts that can be shown don't need special care. But God has put together all the parts of the body. And he has given more honor to the parts that didn't have any. (1 Cor. 12:22–24 NIRV)

Maybe right now your life looks like rocking babies or loading and unloading the dishwasher or doing data entry or welcoming your granddaughter once a week in your Christmas Room. Maybe you're stuck in the deep sad, or maybe you're in the foggy aftermath of sadness. However far removed you are from circumstantial pain and weariness, hopelessness can set in and it can often feel impossible to think about living for Jesus and serving others.

But God is powerful enough to not just comfort us, but sustain us and change us in our weakness. In fact, "His power is made perfect in weakness" (2 Cor. 12:9b). So, whatever you're doing, with whatever gifts and abilities you have, you can do it to the glory of God with the hope of God, even if nothing around you looks or feels hopeful.

Grandma Marlene's kindness to the neighbor down the street, and the guy who fixed her toilet, and the nurse who drew her blood hold special honor. Her nonsensical peace and irrational-looking joy and unshakable "piffle" attitude about the hard parts of life pointed to the beauty and hope of the gospel of Jesus. And how much more beautiful and more stunning is it that those weren't natural qualities in her? How sweet and incredible that her piffle-ness was simply a supernatural work of the Spirit of God?

She really hoped in Jesus, and that's what defined her. She wasn't famous or prominent in any context ever, but the body of Christ can't do without hearts like hers. Weaker, younger saints like me can't do without people like her. Her story was one big "piffle" to the sufferings of this broken world. She didn't submit to fear in her life, because she knew greater was the One who was in her than the one who was in the world (1 John 4:4). She didn't cower to fear death as she got closer to it and lost her husband and son to it, because she knew she was forgiven and accepted by a holy God; she knew death was not final. Joy and peace and piffle were her testimony, through the work of Jesus Christ. What a gift. What a legacy. What an opportunity.

> But he said to me, "My grace is sufficient for you, for my power is perfected in weakness." (2 Cor. 12:9a)

Hope for More Than Forever

My first decade plus of following Jesus was a frequently miserable experience. I was touched by the gospel of Jesus as a teenager, and I knew that I needed Him to save me. I knew that only in Him could I hope for heaven, but I didn't know how to parlay that into present joy. Most of my good works were fear driven and trying to prove something to myself, the people around me, and God.

I observed people like Grandma Marlene and didn't understand what she had that I lacked. I wanted joy and peace, but I so frequently overanalyzed and obsessed over my actions, parsed my motives, and tried to figure out whether or not Jesus would say "Well done" at the end of my life.

Scripture that referenced the narrow path and how few would find it scared me to death.

In Matthew 7, Jesus said,

> "Not everyone who says to me, 'Lord, Lord,' will enter the kingdom of heaven, but only the one who does the will of my Father in heaven. On that day many will say to me, 'Lord, Lord, didn't we prophesy in your name, drive out demons in your name, and do many miracles in your name?' Then I will announce to them, 'I never knew you. Depart from me, you lawbreakers!'" (vv. 21–23)

Terrifying. I'd read that and hear it preached in church and panic over the status of my soul. How could I possibly prove to Jesus that I was the real deal? How could I show myself worthy of being one of His followers?

I couldn't really understand how people like Grandma Marlene existed . . . people who seemed to approach life with inner confidence. I see, now, that her confidence stemmed from being consumed with the goodness of Jesus and forgetful of herself. While I was reading Scripture and obsessing over how well or not well I measured up, she seemed to read it and sing it and study it as though she were enjoying a feast.

I was in it for me, and that's why I lived in fear. She was in it for Jesus Himself, and just as He promised, He gave her peace.

> "Peace I leave with you. My peace I give to you. I do not give to you as the world gives. Don't let your hearts be troubled or fearful." (John 14:27)

And as Grandma aged and I did too, I, of course, noticed that she was flawed, as we all are. But the thing about flawed people who are consistently and authentically following Jesus is that walking with them long-term doesn't make you think, over time, *Wow, they really are awesome superheroes!* or the opposite, *Wow, they actually are the worst!* Instead, people like that, people like Grandma Marlene leave you thinking, *Wow. Jesus is beautiful.*

What a legacy. She lived eighty-eight years, and when I think of her, I don't think of her personal victories or the times she let me down or put her foot in her mouth. I think about how being around her made me understand the love of God. I think about how seeing her faith in action broke through my cynicism in seasons of life when I wasn't walking closely with Jesus. I think about the countless testimonies she shared with me, about Jesus coming through or being present in her life. I think about hope and "oh piffle" peace.

Man, I want to be like that.

I was scheduled to speak at a women's event a few years ago, and the event host asked me to focus on Proverbs 31.

> Strength and honor are her clothing, and she can laugh at the time to come. Her mouth speaks wisdom, and loving instruction is on her tongue. (vv. 25–26)

When I read Proverbs 31:25–26, I don't often think of myself. I do think of Grandma Marlene though. And that's because I'm thinking of the Christlikeness I saw in her life.

I know my husband and my daughters and my soon-to-be-here son will see me struggle. They'll see me get distracted and get discouraged. But I know from witnessing it in people like Grandma and from my own experience of walking with Jesus, that the longer I press in, the more I will be marked by Jesus, and the less I will be marked by my own tendencies.

I want to be someone who is so genuinely following Jesus, that I can say "piffle" at the days to come. I want to be like Grandma.

In loving memory of the radiant Grandma Marlene Esther Jackson, 1933–2021.

Chapter 11

Garden of the Gods vs. The Pool at Hampton Inn

A couple years ago, I went on a work trip to Colorado Springs and happened upon an insanely breathtaking rock formation known as Garden of the Gods. If you've never seen pictures, Google that jank. It's unreal. I stopped my rental car, looked up, and thought I'd found a castle, but no. It was just the tallest, reddest, most unnaturally shaped rock I'd ever seen shooting out of the ground next to me. My jaw dropped like a cartoon all weekend, each time I passed one of the rocks. *I've got to take my girls here*, I remember thinking. A month or so later, I was scheduled to return on another work trip, but this time, I planned to bring my daughters. I was so excited to see them seeing the scenery that took my breath away. I told them what all people tell all other people when witnessing the wonders of nature, "You just can't capture it in a photo. You've got to see it for yourself." So the big day came. We headed to the airport and went over our itinerary for Mommy-work-time and afterward-fun-time. I told the girls we'd have all afternoon to gaze at Garden of the Gods, and all three responded similarly. "That's great . . . but did you notice there's a POOL in our hotel?"

Like Mother like Daughters

Maybe it's easy for me to roll my eyes at my young daughters' discernment. Maybe I've swam in enough hotel pools to know that if you've swam in one, you've swam in 'em all. I've experienced so much more and for so much longer that when my daughters choose chlorine buckets over mountainous majesty, I just want to shout, "WHAT?! IT'S GARDEN OF THE GODS! The experience of standing there is a million times better than wading through the tiny, germy pool at Hampton Inn!"

But I have to remember, they've never seen Garden of the Gods. They haven't seen very much of the world at all, really. At this point in their lives, hotel swimming pools are peak amazement.

I've got to remember their vantage point. Their limited perspective. I've got to remember how very much like them I still am.

Far Too Easily Pleased

In *The Weight of Glory*, C. S. Lewis famously wrote, "It would seem that Our Lord finds our desires not too strong, but too weak. We are half-hearted creatures, fooling about with drink and sex and ambition when infinite joy is offered us, like an ignorant child who wants to go on making mud pies in a slum because he cannot imagine what is meant by the offer of a holiday at the sea. We are far too easily pleased."[14]

Just because my mud pies sound *slightly* more sophisticated than a pool in a chain hotel, they aren't any less muddy. I do the exact same thing.

I crave comforts that aren't comforting, when I have access to the ultimate Comforter. I strive for purpose and importance when the Lord has made His sufficiency so clear. Look again at 2 Corinthians 1:

> Blessed be the God and Father of our Lord Jesus Christ, the Father of mercies and the God of all comfort. He comforts us in all our affliction, so that we may be able to comfort those who are in any kind of affliction, through the comfort we ourselves receive from God. For just as the sufferings of Christ overflow to us, so also through Christ our comfort overflows. (vv. 3–5)

In just those three little verses, God's Word makes it plain: He is the ultimate source of comfort, and He is the giver of our ultimate purpose.

We find all that we hope for in Him, and as a result, we are able to point other people to Him.

It's so beautiful. And somehow so avoidable. Why do we delight in hotel pools when Garden of the Gods is only a few exits away?

Hope for Today

Colossians 3:2 is a verse that's often at the front of my mind: "Set your minds on things above, not on earthly things." I think of that verse regularly because I'm so easily distracted. It's the enemy that wants to keep our minds on what is temporary and unfulfilling and soul crushing. "A thief comes only to steal and kill and destroy. I have come so that they may have life and have it in abundance" (John 10:10).

I so deeply want to raise children who are able to see the beauty and experience the power of God, but I have to remember that just as I'm unable to give my kids red-rock-admiration, salvation is a gift from God—a gift I can't give our children. But I can pray for them, and I can lead them, and I can point them to the hope that's above.

And, I can rest, knowing that God is the giver of good gifts and the One who loves my kids even more than I do.

> For you are saved by grace through faith, and this is not from yourselves; it is God's gift—not from works, so that no one can boast. (Eph. 2:8–9)

When I look out at the world around me, I see health crises, and home crises. I see arguments and awkward moments. Wars and incurable diseases. There's so much that looks hopeless, and it makes so much logical sense to feel hopeless when looking at and living for those things. Right now, I'm so physically uncomfortable. I'm more pregnant now than I was a few chapters ago when I told you about this surprise geriatric pregnancy. I'm never not aware that discomfort (and even pain) is part of life, in this season, as it takes a very specific concoction of drugs and vitamins to keep me functional and hydrated right now. When I think about the physical comfort I crave these days, the pool at the Hampton Inn sounds pretty sweet. Pain makes you desperate, you know? It makes you crave something, anything, that will feel better.

But man, it's so much easier to mentally deal with the physical pain of pregnancy when I zoom out of my current discomfort and look up at the relief that is to come.

My thoughts are never far off from the reality that my mom's cancer is back. Since a few chapters ago, my mom's cough has gotten worse. She moves less. The tumor is still inoperable, and the cancer is still present. What do you do with that information?

I told my husband it almost feels like fiction. Impossible. Like, yes, sure, I know this happens to people. I have known people who died of cancer. I've known people who loved people who have died of cancer. But this is my mom. I've never existed in a world without her in it. And trying to imagine my life without the reality of her being available feels impossible to me.

When we first heard the doctor say "inoperable," my mom shared that my dad's response was that right now, we need an eternal perspective. She even mentioned Colossians 3:2.

When death creeps up so closely in your life, you really have to examine what you believe and decide if you really think it's true. If I really believe that putting faith in Jesus results in an eternity in heaven with Him, then that's where my mom is going. My beautiful, kind, wild mom. She'll be healed. She'll be made whole. She'll be her best, truest, purest self—completely void of sin and sickness. What a strange, incredible thing we believe.

So how can I give in to hopelessness if that is true? I can be sad, for sure. But, how can I be hopeless?

Jesus Grieves and Undoes Death

One of my favorite stories in the Bible is when Jesus raised Lazarus from the dead in John 11.

It happened in Bethany, on the Mount of Olives, which is a modern-day Palestinian town bordering East Jerusalem. Mary (the one who poured perfume on Jesus's feet and wiped them with her hair) shared the news with Jesus, "Lord, the one you love is sick" (John 11:3b). So we know that Jesus and Lazarus were friends.

Jesus responded by saying, "This sickness will not end in death but is for the glory of God, so that the Son of God may be glorified through it" (v. 4).

But the thing is, Lazarus died anyway. He died all the way. Dead, buried, in the grave for days. And we have the end of the story, so we know that Jesus ended up raising him from the dead. But imagine being Mary and Martha. Imagine being the family of Lazarus, during that in-between time—when Lazarus was dead, and Jesus was still out of town.

I identify with that so much. If you're reading this book, you're with me, during this point in history where Jesus has already died and resurrected and promised to come back and make all things new and right and healed and whole and perfect. But we're in the in-between. He can raise the dead, but it feels like He's still out of town.

My mom is dying of cancer right now. And I'm just here . . . living my life. Sitting in the back row at my daughter's 8th grade orientation, wondering how much longer I'll have with my mom. Death is still a thing that takes the people we love. But Jesus will get here. One day he'll be back in town and death won't exist anymore.

That's where Lazarus's loved ones were. The friend they love was dying, was dead, and how can you possibly hope for life for someone when they are dead?

When Jesus got to Lazarus's house, he'd already been dead for four days. Martha said to Jesus, "Lord, if you had been here, my brother wouldn't have died. Yet even now I know that whatever you ask from God, God will give you" (John 11:21–22).

Martha understood that Jesus had power over life and death.

Jesus told her that her brother would rise again, and she thought He meant later, in the afterlife.

Then Jesus said those famous, familiar words, "I am the resurrection and the life. The one who believes in me, even if he dies, will live. Everyone who lives and believes in me will never die" (vv. 25–26).

Do you?

Martha told Him that she believed He was the Messiah (v. 27). And then, there's this whole section about Jesus sharing in the sorrow of death. "Jesus wept" (v. 35).

Jesus knew He was about to raise Lazarus from being four-days dead. Jesus knew about the peanut butter and jelly sandwich. He knew that because He, even as a human walking the earth at a particular time in history, was fully God. Physically weak, emotional, "a man of sorrows" (Isa. 53:3 ESV), and yet without sin, and without the powerlessness that we have, the God-man knew what to do.

After grieving with His friends, Jesus prayed. He talked to God, and commanded Lazarus to "come out" (John 11:43). And a friend was brought back to life.

It's comforting, here in the in-between, to read stories like this one in John 11. It's comforting to remember that, just like Martha, we can claim Jesus as our Messiah, knowing that one day, He will resurrect the saints and restore this broken world back to its original Eden-like perfection.

It's comforting, too, to notice how Mary and Martha both raised their concerns to Jesus ("if you had only been here, Lazarus wouldn't have died" vv. 21, 32). God gives us the freedom to raise our concerns to Him and find comfort in how He responds.

Jesus comforted Martha with the truth and He comforted Mary with His own tears. They received comfort and claimed Jesus as their Messiah in spite of their pain. Like these women, we have freedom to raise our concerns to Jesus, receive His solidarity and comfort in our time of need, and claim Him as Messiah—all at the same time.

Jesus can handle our concerns. And Jesus can do miraculous things. I may not get to see my mom healed and made new before that final resurrection promised to those of us who believe, but the same Jesus who walked this earth and raised His friend Lazarus is now seated at the right hand of God. He'll be back in town. My mom will rise again.

The True Garden of the One True God

When I took my girls to Colorado, my middle daughter asked me, "Why do they call that rock place 'Garden of the Gods'?" I thought about it, and started answering, as I often do, "Well, I'm not sure. We can research it . . . but I'm guessing it's because the rocks are so huge and the people who named these rocks probably imagined giant god-like people walking around and living here, because everything is so enormous."

Non-believing people have been trying to make sense of the majesty of nature since the very beginning. You stand on the edge of the Grand Canyon or next to Mount Everest and can't help but think, *There is something bigger than me . . . grander than me . . . outside of me that must be responsible for all this.*

Theologians call this concept *general revelation*. Meaning, by looking intentionally at creation, it becomes clear that God is revealing Himself to mankind in a general way. You can watch a sunset and have your soul stirred to worship. You can look at the stars and sense a divine being who has the power and creativity to design all that splendor. The sky declares that He's big and sweeping. The smallest flower declares that He's also gentle and lowly. The mountains declare His grandeur and stability. The bazillion species of birds with their bazillion color combinations declare His lavishness and creativity and abounding generosity—because after all, He could have only made one species in one color.

Yet so many people suppress this sensation, and choose to explain away God's obvious vastness, glory, and hugeness by attributing creation to lesser things like giants, man-made "gods," or accidents.

There are so many false hopes and also false gods that we can wrongly set our minds on that will let us down. The "gods" who figuratively could have roamed through the red rocks of Colorado don't have power over death because they are not real.

Jesus is flesh-and-bone real. The real, true God. ". . . the way, the truth, and the life," to put it in His words (John 14:6). The God who created the perfect flourishing garden of Eden is the same God who will restore it.

I used to struggle with the idea of the afterlife. I don't think I'm a visual person. When I close my eyes and try to imagine heaven, I see blackness. I mean, I can remember what Revelation 21–22 says about it, with the jewels and the crystal-clear water and pearly gates, but it's hard to hope in something that is abstract.

What really helped me get excited about eternity was when I learned Jesus promised not only "a new heaven" but also a "new earth."

If you want to get super Old Testamental, read these verses from Ezekiel 36:

> "'This is what the Lord God says: On the day I cleanse you from all your iniquities, I will cause the cities to be inhabited, and the ruins will be rebuilt. The desolate land will

> be cultivated instead of lying desolate in the sight of everyone who passes by. They will say, "This land that was desolate has become like the garden of Eden. The cities that were once ruined, desolate, and demolished are now fortified and inhabited." Then the nations that remain around you will know that I, the LORD, have rebuilt what was demolished and have replanted what was desolate. I, the LORD, have spoken and I will do it.'" (vv. 33–36)

The book of Ezekiel is a strange book. Trust me. Most of the book is full of intense visions and symbols but chapters 33–48 are some of the most hopeful pages of the Bible. The first thirty-two chapters are announcements of God's judgment of Israel because of their idolatry. But—and I'll let an expert say it—"the very arrangement of the book with the announcement of judgments in the beginning and the declaration of restoration at the end suggests that Ezekiel's message is ultimately one of hope."[15] Of course it is. God promises His people renewal and restoration, including a new temple (chapters 40–42) and a restored people (chapter 47) "following the new David" (that's Jesus), and this is all happening in a place that "has become like the garden of Eden."[16] Even the Old Testament prophets of doom can't help but be hopeful in the kingdom of God.

When I think about Eden, God's original perfect design for humans, I think about the most beautiful mountains I've ever seen, but on steroids. I think about new life. Perfection.

If you read through the first few chapters of Genesis, it's such a beautiful description. The land was flourishing, the people were flourishing. God gave Adam work to do. That was pre-sin, pre-curse. Work was a beautiful and fulfilling part of life. The Bible says that the trees were beautiful and had delicious food on them. Everything was right.

> Then God planted a garden in Eden, in the east. He put the Man he had just made in it. God made all kinds of trees grow from the ground, trees beautiful to look at and good to eat. The Tree-of-Life was in the middle of the garden, also the Tree-of-Knowledge-of-Good-and-Evil.
>
> A river flows out of Eden to water the garden and from there divides into four rivers. The first is named Pishon; it flows through Havilah where there is gold. The gold of this land is good. The land is also known for a sweet-scented resin and the onyx stone. The second river is named Gihon; it flows through the land of Cush. The third river is named Hiddekel and flows east of Assyria. The fourth river is the Euphrates.
>
> God took the Man and set him down in the Garden of Eden to work the ground and keep it in order. (Gen. 2:8–15 MSG)

My favorite nature spot when we lived in California was this mini-beach in Corona del Mar. It felt like a secret, private stretch of beauty that no one knew about apart from a few. You had to park on one of the streets named after flowers off of the Pacific Coast Highway. My favorite was Poppy Street. You'd park on the road and walk by the mansions with the beautiful flower gardens and ornate gates. The flowers were perfectly kept and bursting with color. Then, you'd try to maintain your composure as you came down the hill and walked on the rocky shore of the Pacific Ocean. Giant black rocks shot up out of the ocean. Sea glass peeked out through the pebbles and sand. The air felt like magic—perfectly cool, not cold. But as stunning as it was to be there, it wasn't perfect. The rocks were full of crabs that scared my youngest. The undertow could wrench you out into an endless, churning sea if you stepped in the wrong part of the water at the wrong time. The people visiting were in pain, all of us, in one way or another. It's hard to even imagine being in beautiful nature, but void of things that bite, void of memories that haunt, void of hypothetical fears. But that's what Adam and Eve had in Eden. And that's the kind of life we'll get to experience when God remakes the earth.

I'm not sure what will be happening in my personal life next time I visit Colorado's Garden of the Gods or the little beach in Corona del Mar, but I know something will be off. Someone I love will be hurting. The presence of someone I want will be absent.

But there is a real, true garden of the one true God, and there we will get to enjoy creation that doesn't die, that doesn't groan, and that doesn't have an end date. There will be nothing separating us from each other or from our Father or from the saints who have already passed.

> For I consider that the sufferings of this present time are not worth comparing with the glory that is going to be revealed to us. For the creation eagerly waits with anticipation for God's sons to be revealed. For the creation was subjected to futility—not willingly, but because of him who subjected it—in the hope that the creation itself will also be set free from the bondage to decay into the glorious freedom of God's children. For we know that the whole creation has been groaning together with labor pains until now. Not only that, but we ourselves who have the Spirit as the firstfruits—we also groan within ourselves, eagerly waiting for adoption, the redemption of our bodies. (Rom. 8:18–23)

We groan because the garden of God is a real place where we will really get to live. In fact, the Bible says this garden won't merely be in the primitive state it was when Adam and Eve roamed the premises; it will be even better. It will be fully developed into everything Eden should have developed into. It will be something more like a Garden-City, ornate gates and all. No longer will there be an angel with a sword guarding the Tree of Life. We will be resurrected, glorified, and immortal. Nature will be peaceful and flourishing and healthy. The majesty and transcendence and love we experience now will be fully realized and never failing. Until then, we take our time at the Hampton Inn. And we hold on to hope.

Chapter 12

A Sick Donkey on a Saturday

One thing I've learned as an adult-onset farmer is that while farm living is bursting with harvest and life, it is also no stranger to death. When you're raising livestock, the cloud of death is inevitable, as predators threaten to disturb peaceful pastures and continue the circle of life.

We started with chickens. Then dogs and cats. Then, we got a donkey to protect our chickens, and an additional donkey (the mini-one who almost yee-hawed Dewy and me to death) to be friends with our protector donkey (donkeys do best in pairs). Things were going great until one of our donkeys (the mini) recently got really sick—sick really fast.

The day we learned he was sick, after several check-ins, my youngest said she couldn't watch. Later that day, I told her I was going to check on the donkey and she said, "Is he dead? Let me know if he's dead. If he is, I can't go out there and see. I just never want to see him again. But if he's okay, I'll come out."

My eight-year-old's response to the concept of death reminded me so much of mine. When faced with sickness, death, and pain, I just want to look away. I want to stay up in my room and hide because it's too horrible a thing.

During seasons of grief, I've often thought, *How do people do life without Jesus?*

Death is too terrible to comprehend. It is somehow both shocking and inevitable. But Jesus didn't look away. He walked toward death, not wanting but willing to face it and defeat it forever. Sick livestock and pet funerals and people funerals break our hearts, and the enemy uses those things to try to make us feel hopeless. But the cross of Christ—and especially His resurrection—gives us back our hope.

> He will wipe away every tear from their eyes. Death will be no more; grief, crying and pain will be no more, because the previous things have passed away. Then the one seated on the throne said, "Look, I am making everything new." He also said, "Write, because these words are faithful and true." (Rev. 21:4–5)

I was at Sunday school this past week, and we just so happened to be looking at Revelation 21, and I loved the picture our workbook painted of what we have to hope for after this life:

> When Christ returns and the children of God are revealed, the creation itself will be made new. Like the resurrected bodies that Christians will one day receive, the physical world itself will undergo a similar

> transformation, so much so that the Scriptures describe it as a new heaven and a new earth (2 Pet. 3:13). Scripture describes the new earth as a city (Rev. 21:10–11, 21–26) and as a physical place that will include eating and drinking (Luke 22:18; Rev. 19:9). Best of all, Christ will be all in all, and we shall see Him face to face.[17]

Our teacher asked what we were looking forward to in the new heavens and new earth. Some joked about reflecting on the conversation we were having in the circle of chairs.

"I wonder if we'll remember talking about this."

One man said, "I think I'll be surprised about how wrong my assumptions were . . . and also how right they were."

People talked about reuniting with loved ones who had passed or meeting relatives who'd gone before them that they'd only heard about. One man talked about going on vacation with family friends, and sitting around laughing and talking, and that feeling of being sad that the vacation was ending and that everyone would leave and go back home. Then he said, "I imagine heaven won't have that feeling, because we'll never have to leave."

We talked about how hard it is to even try to comprehend the best parts of this life without the sadness of impending loss attached to them. We can't comprehend it because every good thing we enjoy has an expiration date.

We'll get to enjoy the best things of this life—eating and drinking, togetherness with the saints, and like the workbook said, "best of all," Christ, face to face, with us fully and forever.

The Bible study book went on to quote J. Scott Duvall saying, "The old priestly blessing/prayer for the Lord to 'make his face shine on you' and 'turn his face toward you' (Num. 6:25–26) finds its ultimate fulfillment here. God's people will also bear his 'name,' meaning they will belong to him, imitate his character, and live safely in his presence."[18]

Have you had an "experiencing God" moment here on earth? I have. There's nothing better. There's nothing like it. But now we only get glimpses of what it will be like to be fully in His perfect presence, no longer suffering from the curse of sin.

When Tim Keller passed away recently, I couldn't stop crying. He was one of my favorite pastor/author/speakers, and to think of him not being here really made me sad. His books and sermons changed my life. They helped me understand that the gospel isn't just a someday hope for peace, but the hope for peace in life right now, today. I remember, after the sadness and shock passed, just feeling so grateful to have been alive at the same time he was. Later that day, I opened one of my Grandma Marlene's old Bibles that my mom let me keep. Grandma had highlighted a few verses in red and this was one of them . . .

> For now we see in a mirror dimly, but then face to face. Now I know in part; then I shall know fully, even as I have been fully known. (1 Cor. 13:12 ESV)

I was heartbroken when Tim Keller died, and then supremely heartbroken when Grandma Marlene died. But looking at her red pencil highlight of that verse in that black leather Bible filled me with hope as I reflected on the truth of what Scripture said—now, we see dimly, but also now, Tim Keller and Grandma Marlene see in full. Healed, whole, forever. Thank You, Lord.

Why Do the Mountains Make Us Sad?

Black Mountain, North Carolina, is so beautiful, it hurts my eyes. We just had a little family getaway there—mini-golf in the woods, biscuits from our favorite breakfast place, inhaling the crisp, mountain air, walking through creeks and waterfalls and foresty pathways. It's just otherworldly.

Right before it was time to say goodbye to the mountain we were staying on, we drove to the very top so we could stand at the lookout. It was an explosion of beauty as we witnessed blue mountains and valleys that looked like they went on forever.

We took a family picture, my husband prayed, and we headed back to the car to drive down and return our hotel key.

My youngest opened her car door and said, "Why does seeing the mountains make me sad?"

This led to a beautiful answer from my beautiful husband who reminded us that seeing the majesty of untouched nature reminds us that this world was made perfectly—that the mountains were there way before us and will remain way after we're gone. They remind us that creation was built to be everlasting, but we live so much of our lives in pain and distracted by what's temporary.

Impatiently, I nudged my husband, "Get to the happy part!"

The beauty for believers is that someday God will remake those Blue Ridge Mountains and He'll remake us too. We'll experience immortality forever and ever amen, and so will they.

"So, we won't be sad when we look at mountains anymore?" one of my other daughters said.

No. Nothing will make us sad, ever again. When the mountains make you sad, remember and remind your people that we carry the hope of eternal life, eternal joy, and indestructible, forever mountains.

The mountains here may eventually crumble, just like our bodies, but the love of Jesus, who gives us eternity, can never be taken away.

> "Though the mountains move
> and the hills shake,
> my love will not be removed from you
> and my covenant of peace will not be
>   shaken,"
> says your compassionate Lord. (Isa. 54:10)

What a reality. We really can be joyful, peaceful people. You'd think that the longer life goes, the more difficult it is to get lost in delight, but I think that when God's Word says, "Taste and see that the Lord is good. How happy is the person who takes refuge in him!" (Ps. 34:8), it's true. I think when

God says we can be happy in His refuge, in His goodness, we can! Life was painful and tragic back when David wrote that psalm too.

Apparently, Psalm 34 was written during the time in King David's life when he was running from King Saul, afraid of Saul, afraid for his life and afraid of the king of Gath, Abimelech (also known as Achish). You can read about it all in 1 Samuel 21, but when we look at the corresponding psalm, we can see David's faith, His dependence on the Lord, and even his happiness. It's hard for me to imagine being in David's position—being chased, fearing being killed, and yet able to pray a prayer like he did in Psalm 34. But, then again, isn't that just so the Christian life? We are all facing hard things. We all live hurting. We all have an enemy chasing us down. We all get weary. Yet there is our God every step of the way: good, holy, righteous, near to the brokenhearted.

In verses 4–5, David writes, "I sought the LORD, and he answered me and rescued me from all my fears. Those who look to him are radiant with joy . . ."

God, make this true of us.

What do you do with a word like "hope" when life keeps providing a seemingly never-ending stream of disappointments? What do you do when your relationships end or leave? When home doesn't feel like home anymore? When what you thought and planned for your life ends up not only not happening, but becoming painful and sad?

The answer must be this: You stop living for this life. You know, that thing Jesus said to do all along? I think that. I think maybe if we'd been living for eternity all along, the disappointments of this life wouldn't sting so much. Those who look to him are radiant with joy.

Away from Home

Have you ever had a bad vacation? Maybe you were visiting some distant relatives and you're on an air mattress in not-your-favorite-city and you're uncomfortable with the various tensions in the house. But you tell yourself, *It's okay. I'm going home on Tuesday.*

What if we lived our lives like that? What if we lived our lives in light of the fact that we get to go home soon? Not the idealized home we're all seeking here on earth, but a real, stable, eternal home. A place where tension doesn't exist and relationships are never disappointing?

I think maybe I've been struggling because I've so wanted this earth, this home, to feel more like a home away from home. Like, consciously, I've known that this world is not my true home, but maybe if I get the right people around me—people who never offend, people who never leave—and maybe if I fix everything up real nice, this earth-home can fill my longing.

But it just doesn't work.

Brandon and I have often reflected on the last time we felt like our lives made sense.

We were at a big party at my friend, Caroline's, house. Our pastor was there. Our friends were there. All felt right in our little world. Brandon and I would often say, "We're going to do life with these people in this city at this church until we're dead."

But we didn't. Our friends moved away. We moved away.

Family died. Uncle Jimmy and Grandma were gone. Everything happy felt like it had a dark cloud over it.

I'll never live in a world with all the people I love at arm's reach again. I'll never be naive enough again to say, "We're going to do life with these people in this city at this church until we're dead."

What a sad and lonely realization, right? I've suffered disappointments and trauma since my childhood, but something about the loss of those friends and that party and those stand-in parents, Uncle Jimmy and Grandma Marlene, did something to me.

Have you ever done that thing with your people where you describe them in a few words? My husband has always included the word *indefatigable* when talking about me. Sometimes he'd switch it up and say "unsinkable." But as I found myself depressed, giant, pregnant, and lonely the last year, I said to Brandon through tired tears, "I'm not indefatigable anymore. I'm not unsinkable. I think I've sunk."

My dad has always said that my mom and I share an "irrational exuberance" for life. The catchphrase hasn't fit me lately, but overall, yes. Historically, when I have found myself in the "depths of despair,"[19] to quote Anne of Green Gables, the Lord has broadened my view, set my heart on Him, and restored my hope. Maybe my dad is right. Maybe exuberance on earth is irrational. Or maybe joyfulness in the face of pain is a gift of the gospel that we all have access to.

You're not alone. I'm not alone. And I hope that through these stories, you can clearly see again the One who made it so. One of Jesus's names, Immanuel, means "God with us." We're not alone, because God came here, to our home away from home.

You know when you visit the home of someone with wild, screaming toddlers and you're like, *What am I doing here, when I could be somewhere that's not here with people who are larger and not screaming?*

Well, God took a seat on the figurative dirty, sticky couch of our chaotic home. He stepped into our dysfunction, our childishness, and He stayed until the job was done. Remember 1 Peter 1? We've looked at it a couple times throughout this book. I'll put it in front of you again:

> Because of his great mercy he has given us new birth into a living hope through the resurrection of Jesus Christ from the dead and into an inheritance that is imperishable, undefiled, and unfading, kept in heaven for you. (vv. 3–4)

We have hope that is alive and an inheritance forever.

So let's hold onto hope in a world that so often looks hopeless. Let's laugh at the days to come like the children of God we are—cared for, loved, eternal people who know how this story ends. As Tim Keller said, "Only when our greatest love is God, a love that we cannot lose even in death, can we face all things with peace. Grief was not to be eliminated but seasoned and buoyed up with love and hope."[20]

Everything. New.[21]

My middle daughter was born without ears. We adopted Joy at almost four, and when the Vanderbilt genius doctors said they could build ears for her, she lit up like a Christmas tree. The original plan was for three surgeries within one year to give her a set of printed custom ears, covered in her own harvested skin, that would last for her lifetime. But just a few months ago, she had her sixth ear surgery. One year turned to four and three surgeries turned to six, as Joy's unique anatomy introduced complications, which led to revisions. What we hoped might be over relatively quickly became complex and painful. At one point, earlier this year, we thought Joy would have to permanently lose one of her ears. We were praying surgery number six would save the day.

But sometimes there are things we suffer—things we have to watch our children suffer—that don't have solutions. Like my wise counselor reminded me back on page 78, you can't always tie a pretty bow around the sad thing.

Sometimes, children get sick, lose body parts, lose people they love, or have to say goodbye to sick donkeys. And what is there to say in those moments, those seasons, those years? What is there to do?

During the weeks that we thought Joy would lose her ear, I remember sitting at the foot of her bed one night and crying with her because she was understandably crestfallen and I couldn't fix it. I couldn't save her ear or protect her from the pain of the surgery or the embarrassment of the loss. But what I did have for her was the living hope I carry. Hope that the groans of this life can't compare to. What I can share is the help of the Savior who loves her right now and the future hope of healing and wholeness that Joy will experience when her painful past is washed away, and her mind and body are made completely new.

Joy's journey of health and home has frequently forced our family to cling to the hope of Jesus in a way we might not if all our plans panned out and if all our ideas of wholeness were found here on a fallen earth. I hate seeing my daughter suffer, but the beautiful depth of faith that it has produced in her at such a young age is striking. I'm grateful that I can point my girls and my own forgetful heart to the One seated on the throne. The Powerful Maker of New. The One who keeps His promises. The One whose sacrifice ended our hopelessness. The only One who can take broken things and make them over again. The only One who can make dead things alive forever. No matter what you or your family face today, look at the cross. Look a little longer at the empty tomb. Look at the Eternal Savior who promises, "I am coming soon." He is. He is coming soon and pain and death are trembling.

Chapter 13

Terminal Cancer and a Holy Sprinkled Donut

I brought balloons to my mom's final cancer treatment, nine years ago. She's always been the family balloon bringer, so it seemed appropriate to celebrate the life of the family with bright colors and happy helium.

Her cancer was stage three, and when she rang the bell, we celebrated. She was happy and healed. Her hair grew back, and life went back to normal. For nine years.

The Testimony of the Holy Spirit in Action

On the actual day we got the news that my mom's cancer was back, I met my mom and dad at their house. I explained things to my daughters, and before we even saw my parents, we had a good cry. But when we got to the house, my parents were happy. Attentive. Joyful. Full of peace.

I've followed Jesus for twenty-plus years, by now. I shouldn't be surprised when His people are ruled by the power of His Spirit. I shouldn't be surprised when He gives the gifts of joy and peace to the people who have every reason to feel anything but. But it's striking. It's always striking.

The thing is, my parents weren't acting like nothing bad was happening. It wasn't a denial or heads in the clouds.

My mom wrote a song about it—because she's always writing things—and one of the lines was, "Hallelujah, I'm almost home."

I asked her, "Are you at all worried or sad?"

And she looked up for a minute, and then back at me and smiled, "No, I'm not."

And I believe her.

One of the days I went to go see her, when we were still waiting on test results, she had a balloon tied to her chair. I asked her if it was from my sister, and she said, "No, I bought it for myself."

My mom is determined to live her life with joy, and it's not because she's ignorant. It's because she's the opposite. She's being more realistic about the Christian life than those of us who are wringing our hands over her diagnosis. She's walking in faith, living in light of eternity. She knows she's going to live forever.

When the doctors or the world says, "Life is hopeless," God's Word says that our lives are like a vapor, but that our future is eternal and secure.

> Yet you do not know what tomorrow will bring—what your life will be! For you are like vapor that appears for a little while, then vanishes. (James 4:14)

> "My sheep hear my voice, I know them, and they follow me. I give them eternal life, and they will never perish. No one will snatch them out of my hand. My Father, who has given them to me, is greater than all. No one is able to snatch them out of the Father's hand." (John 10:27–29)

So why is it so crazy when people who possess the Holy Spirit live like they possess the Holy Spirit?

When someone is close to heaven, right around the corner, it often reveals what they really believe. What an example. What a testimony it is to see my parents face something so sad and broken and hopeless-looking with peace.

My parents have been students of God's Word for their whole lives. They faithfully study Scripture and it is buried deep in their minds and hearts. They've both been through a lot, and suffered a lot, and in a worldly sense, it would make sense for them to lose hope and be cynical. But here, in the midst of a family crisis, I see the fruit of their faithfulness to Jesus pouring out, comforting everyone around them, when they are the ones suffering most.

Grief on the News

It's a strange added layer of grief, when not only do you learn your mom is dying of terminal cancer, but so does the media. A few days after we got the news and my mom shared it on her Instagram, the internet picked up the story, and suddenly, every news site and app and social media feed was filled with headlines citing my mom's terminal cancer and quoting her video announcement, but subtracting her levity and humor.

> *"SNL" alum Victoria Jackson battles inoperable cancer that could eventually "suffocate" her "to death."*[22]
>
> *Former Saturday Night Live Star Reveals Terminal Cancer Battle*[23]
>
> *"Saturday Night Live" Alum Shares Devastating Health Update*[24]

My sister and I sat on the phone for almost two hours the night the news articles came out. We cried, we laughed, we talked through all the what-ifs.

And then it was Saturday morning and my daughters reminded us that it was Dunkin Donut day.

We rolled out of bed and into the parking spot at Dunkin and I felt a wave of sadness rush over me. I remembered running into my mom at that same Dunkin Donuts, just before we moved to California.

I tried to be a normal, functioning mom in Dunkin. I really did. I wiped away a few tears from under my glasses, placed our order, and sat down with my family. But I couldn't hold it in. Tears turned into more tears and then my face did that thing, you know, when you go from just light, hide-able crying to embarrassing, over-the-top crying? It was clearly a fun donut run. As that started happening to me, I told

Brandon, "I'm sorry. I can't be in public right now. I'll wait in the car. Can you give me your keys?" As I started to walk out, I experienced a holy moment with my family in that Dunkin Donuts.

Before I could get to the door, a teenage girl came up to me and said, "I could see that you are sad, so I ordered you a chocolate donut with sprinkles."

I started crying even more and asked her what her name was and she said, "Ava." I could barely talk. I only said, "Thank you Ava," and then a thirty-eight-year-old, heartbroken pregnant woman hugged a kind teenage girl we don't know in Dunkin.

Then Ava said, "Sometimes God tells me to do things, and I just wanted to give you a donut and tell you that you are beautiful and today can be a good day."

The interaction was simple and sweet and I ate that chocolate donut with sprinkles unto the Lord. And we will remember the Ava donut forever.

Thank God for Ava and the guidance of the Holy Spirit. She couldn't know the magnitude of the moment in our lives she was stepping into. But the Spirit of God guided her to encourage me with a few kind words and a donut. It was like our family got a hug from heaven in a season of sadness.

It's really hard to put into words how powerful that small act of kindness was for my heart. When I started writing this book this year, I wasn't quite sure how I was going to do it. I wasn't quite sure I was going to point people to hope, when I was feeling so deficient in it myself. These months have been marked by so much physical weakness. The last few years have been filled with devastating news of death and loss. And here's the thing.

God knew all of this. God, who is only good and only loving and always perfect, knew that this world, broken by sin and plagued with pain, was going to press me from all angles. He knew all the ways I'd struggle in my heart. He knew about the nights I'd wrestle with doubt. And like the loving Father that He is, He knew that He would provide for me. He knew that comfort and assurance and understanding would come. That it would chase me down when my body and my mind were too tired. He knew that Comfort and Love would see me crying in a donut shop, and send someone filled by His spirit to remind me that I'm not alone. Like sweet Ava said, "Today can be a good day."

That day was a good day. I ate a donut I didn't even plan on having that day—and with sprinkles on top. I texted with my mom, and she said that the medicine the doctor gave her helped her get eleven hours of sleep that night.

That day, the Spirit of the living God reminded me through His work in a teenage girl that love never dies. Love is powerful enough to make a hopeless-feeling, old pregnant lady remember to hope.

A Song About a Song for Uncle Jimmy

When I was around twelve, Uncle Jimmy gave me one of his old guitars and taught me how to play a few chords. We were living in LA that year, and he'd come over and show me things, and then I'd practice and sing the songs back to him next time he came by.

He always loved the Beatles, so one of the first songs he ever taught me was "Here, There, and Everywhere." I'll never forget a lyric from it—the one that talks about how each of us tends to keep believing that love never dies.

When he died, I remembered that song, and I remembered feeling like his death was so wrong. But I think, on a soul level, we all know that love never dies. When you love someone, that love doesn't just go away, even when the person goes away.

I wrote this to Jimmy, shortly after he died. Call it a poem, or an unfinished song. It's what came out.

You taught me how to play a Beatles song on
your guitar.
And I still remember the first few lines.
It went "Here and there and everywhere,"
And something about how love never dies.
Love never dies.

Where'd you go?
I don't remember the part that comes after.
Why'd you show so much love to me
And then give it up
In the pain of life?

Now your guitar's propped against my wall
With a broken string
And I don't know how to fix it.
You never taught me that.

The weighty aftermath of a person's suicide on their remaining loved ones is so painful. When death happens naturally, it still feels tragic, but it is easier to rest in the sovereignty of God, and remember His power over life and death. But when someone's life is taken, by themselves or someone else, there's so much left that feels unfinished. The love doesn't die.

Love That Did Die

If you look in the Bible, you learn what real love is. You learn *who* love is.

> And we have come to know and to believe the love that God has for us. God is love, and the one who remains in love remains in God, and God remains in him. (1 John 4:16)

We, as human beings, only know what love is because of the example of Jesus. Jesus humbled Himself, gave of Himself, and had compassion on His enemies. And because of His outrageous act of love, we have peace with God and a future with God and the ability to love and encourage the hurting people in this hurting world, the way Ava the donut girl loved and encouraged me.

> Therefore, since we have been justified through faith, we have peace with God through our Lord Jesus Christ, through whom we have gained access by faith into this grace in which we now stand. And we boast in the hope of

> the glory of God. Not only so, but we also glory in our sufferings, because we know that suffering produces perseverance; perseverance, character; and character, hope. And hope does not put us to shame, because God's love has been poured out into our hearts through the Holy Spirit, who has been given to us. (Rom. 5:1–5 NIV)

Because God Himself, Love itself, chose to die for us, we are able to persevere. We are able to hope. We are able to love others.

When I first set out to write this book, I was planning on writing ten chapters. A nice round number. I had my stories and my outline planned out. But this year didn't turn out as I planned it, so neither did my outline. Ten chapters became twelve.

After my encounter with Ava and her donut, I decided this book needed one more chapter, and it became thirteen. Rather than ending on the hope we have for after death, I decided we should end on the hope and love we are able to pass on to others because of what Jesus has done for us. That's literally why we're alive. It's why we're here.

When you're walking through tragedies and heartaches, it's so easy to get internally focused. It's so easy to get so stuck in your own pain that you don't feel like it's even possible to be able to look outward and love and encourage others.

Ava reminded me what a joy, what a gift it is when a hurting human loves another hurting human in the name of

Christ. To see the need and walk toward it, rather than holing up in your house and looking away.

I don't know Ava's story. I don't know what has caused her pain in her life. But I know that no living being can walk through this world unscathed. If she isn't hurting yet, she will be. We are all hurting. We are all confused. We all have seasons when we know we're not crushing it. But that doesn't disqualify us from being people who love each other. That doesn't disqualify us from spreading hope to a hurting world.

I was so moved by Ava's action. So was my husband. That Sunday, he shared about it in his sermon at our church, and he relayed that he stayed behind as I walked to the car to thank Ava and her friend. He told them that we had found out recently my mom is dying of cancer and Ava began to cry. And he told her we were Christians and thanked her for listening to the Lord and being willing to encourage our family in Dunkin Donuts. And her friend hugged her, and they just began to cry together.

Then he shared with our church what made Ava's willingness to love a stranger so powerful. It was powerful because it was so biblical, maybe more biblical than Ava could even articulate right now.

Ava told me God led her to me, and she told me I am beautiful. I was reminded that I am fearfully and wonderfully made at a time when it would be natural to wonder about the goodness of God.

And she said that day could be a good day. So true. Every day is the day that the Lord has made and we can rejoice and be glad in it (Ps. 118:24). Even the sad days. Any day can be the day the Holy Spirit sends a small reminder of His kindness by guiding a fifteen-year-old girl to give a donut to a weeping woman with a word of encouragement in the name of the Lord.

Mark 9:41 says, "Whoever gives you a cup of water to drink in my name, because you belong to Christ—truly I tell you, he will never lose his reward."

I was encouraged and convicted by Ava and her donut, and I hope you are too. I hope God makes me more like Ava who was in a donut shop with her friends and saw a sad woman and asked God what He wanted her to do. We, too, can ask God to guide us in hope to give hope.

Man, I thank the Lord for Ava and people like her. I thank Him because sometimes, reading about something or hearing about something isn't enough to get you to change course. Sometimes you need to be the recipient of an undeserved, unexpected gift, in order to be moved to change.

Ava's donut was a spark that reminded me of the most magnificent spark any human can experience when we experience salvation.

Because the love of God brings dead things to life. The love of God makes broken things new. The love of God, whether expressed in the ultimate way through a Savior on a cross, or in a smaller way through a teen with a donut, is powerful enough to flood a hopeless heart with hope. Sure, some days your hope might feel more hopeful-ish but for those of us who are on, what the late Eugene Peterson called "a long obedience in the same direction,"[25] our hope doesn't have to stay an "ish." In fact, it won't. It can't.

Because those things we hope for—healing, carrying, life everlasting, restoration and peace—those things are promised to us. They are right around the corner. And we can taste and see glimpses of them right now, in this life, whether it be through the thoughtfulness of a teenager, or in the inexplicable peace of a mom. We see glimpses of heaven touching earth all around us, if we're looking.

I asked my mom, again, this week if she was sad or scared. She said no in the moment, but texted me later, the most beautiful text.

> I've been thinking all night about your good questions: Am I scared or sad? When you asked, the kids were listening and I seemed flippant. The truth is, I'm so sad missing my kids/grandkids next adventures that if I let myself feel it, I'd slip into a depression so deep I would die now. So, I think about Bible verses, the big picture, and what Jesus would do. He cried, 'Let this cup pass from Me, but Your will be done.' I'll see you soon in heaven. Also God could do a miracle or come back! Tell the grandkids, yes, I'm sad. I love them more than anything, but God has a plan better than we could imagine. And, I'm alive now! Let's party!

Can you even believe that text? Can you even believe those words?

She keeps hoping and I'm going to keep sharing, because we all need the comfort of this rich faith my mom is carrying.

I was so taken aback. Maybe even more so by the peace and joy she was exhibiting. I told her how much she amazed me. I told her what I've already told you: that I shouldn't be surprised that Jesus is giving her an eternal mindset of peace and joy after she's spent so much of her life trying to follow and worship Him. I told her what a beautiful and convicting thing it is to witness. As my family is watching my mom die, right now, as I finish this book, we're watching a woman for whom death has lost its sting.

Let's finish where we started. First Peter 1:3–5 says,

> Blessed be the God and Father of our Lord Jesus Christ. Because of his great mercy he has given us new birth into a living hope through the resurrection of Jesus Christ from the dead and into an inheritance that is imperishable, undefiled, and unfading, kept in heaven for you. You are being guarded by God's power through faith for a salvation that is ready to be revealed in the last time.

What a truth, today and forever, that God has given us new birth into a living hope through the resurrection of Jesus Christ from the dead. Hope is a gift.

Maybe that's the first and last thing we must settle if we want hope. We can't make our own hope because we can't make new birth. We can only receive it. We can't earn hope, because we can't earn salvation, we can only get it as a gift.

As much as we want hope, as much as we know we need it, hope is not a program we can participate in. If there was a podcast series about how to achieve hope, it would probably just be someone reading Romans 15:13 over and over again:

> Now may the God of hope fill you with all joy and peace as you believe so that you may overflow with hope by the power of the Holy Spirit. Now may the God of hope fill you with all joy and peace as you believe so that you may overflow with hope by the power of the Holy Spirit. Now may the God of hope fill you . . .

It is living hope right now. It is living hope forever. It is hope today and beyond the flimsy grave, in Jesus.

I think this is where I want to end this book. Here, as I look at my phone and wonder when it's going to be my dad calling to tell me that my mom's not here anymore. Here, as I await the birth of the son I didn't plan on having. Here, where death and life track side by side. Here, in this so painful, so broken, so sad, yet so beautiful world, I carry this unsinkable hope with me. I have a life vest for the soul. I have a hope and an inheritance and a peace I don't deserve. Hope that God is real. Hope that He will carry us. Hope that death is coming for the deep sad. Hope that in our weakness, He intercedes. Hope that His Word, His Son, His Sacrifice is true. Hope that Eden is returning all over again.

Hope means it won't always be this way. As my mom always says, with the greatest amount of exclamation points possible, "YAY JESUS!!!!!!!!!!!"

> Now may the God of hope fill you with all joy and peace as you believe so that you may overflow with hope by the power of the Holy Spirit. (Rom. 15:13)

Acknowledgments

Brandon, you know, more than anyone else, that none of this would exist without you. You have helped make all my dreams come true, from helping me outline my ideas, to taking time out of your work schedule to edit every article and book and Instagram post I write. You have been the "wind beneath my wings" for wow, eighteen years now, and you are still my best friend. These books wouldn't exist without all the Brandonness you sprinkle in, especially this one. Thank you for bringing more hope and more light and more gospel into these pages. I'm grateful. And I love you so much.

My children! Ever, you are incredible. You are wise beyond your years and our long talks are my favorite thing about you being this age. I love your studiousness and how seriously you follow Jesus. I love your incredible sense of humor and how much you love reading! What a blessed mom I am to have you as my firstborn. Joy, for the past seven years of knowing you, I have learned so much about Jesus through the way you live. You are supernaturally selfless, unbelievably resilient, and so helpful. Thank you for working so hard in everything you do and looking out for your family the way you do. You are a gift from God to our family. Dewy, you are just the most snuggly, sweet delight to our family. Your preciousness and love for life make our home a happy place, and I just love the way God made my Dewy-nug. Girls, remember the day Mommy and Daddy finished editing this book and we hired you as house cleaners? You crushed it so hard. You three are amazing. I am so thankful I get to be your mommy. And Sweet Baby James! You are here and you are the best baby in the whole world! As I'm writing these acknowledgments, you are currently strapped to my chest in the baby carrier that my editor, Ashley, gave me at your shower. You were the surprise burst of life and hope we didn't know we needed. All year, I was focused on my own pain and sickness, and then you arrived, and I told everyone, I would do it all over a million times. I love you so much and I can't imagine our family without you.

To my baby biscuit, Aubrey, my sister, my forever friend. I'm so proud of the woman you are and so thankful for your presence in my life. Let's get another matching tattoo soon. Bam Bam and Papa, you're the greatest grandparents on earth. I love you and thank you for loving me and our family and for always, through thick and thin, pointing me to Jesus as our one and only hope. To my family through marriage—Lala, Brian, Gran, Pops, Norma, Great Papa—what a gift it is to be in a family of faith. Thank you for your love and kindness and constant prayers.

Katie and Vanessa, you two were constant, patient, lovely, and wonderful friends to me throughout all the heartaches I documented in this book. Thank you for listening to hours of me venting. Thank you for speaking truth to me when I battled hopelessness and confusion. I do not deserve friends like you and I thank God for you.

To the people in SoCal, who loved me so well when you barely knew me. I will never forget your kindness. Manley family—you sent me a succulent garden when you heard Uncle Jimmy died, and it arrived at my door the day Grandma Marlene died. It stayed alive for three years. Diane and Samantha, you embraced me and my girls like we were your own and brought us so much joy. Geigers, you have been so good to us over the years. We are so thankful for your love and for leading us to so much good. There are so many others. Kim, Donna, Rachel, and all the wonderful people from our HB CC family and at Mariners. You made California feel like home the brief time I was there. I will love you forever!

To my people in Tennessee, who brought us right back into the fold. Katrina and Caroline and Mattie and Bev and so many more. I am so thankful for friends like you.

Thank you, Ashley Gorman. First of all thank you for the amazing baby carrier that I'm holding James in right now as I go over all your wise and beautiful edits. What a gift to work with you on a third project! You are so brilliant and so sweet and so stunningly beautiful! I appreciate you making my work better and what a blessing our Mexican restaurant catch-ups are to me. You are full of wisdom and compassion, and I am grateful to have such a talented editor who often feels more like a friend. You REALLY put the work in on this book, and people will never know how much beauty and wisdom you added. God knows. I'm so thankful for you.

Mary Wiley, you have been another publishing constant since the very beginning. I'm so grateful for your wisdom and friendship and availability in my life. You're amazing and I'm so thankful for you and proud of you, as I look at all the amazing work you've been putting into the world these past few years. You're a blessing to your readers and your coworkers and your family and to me.

And thank you, reader. It never gets lost on me that I get to do this. That I get to process through pain and life and joy and confusion with Jesus and with you. Getting to meet so many of you through my travels, and connecting with you online, hearing you share your testimonies has been such a comfort and gift to me. Thank you for caring to read the things I write and for feeling like friends. I'm very thankful for you.

About the Author

Scarlet Hiltibidal is the author of *Afraid of All the Things, You're the Worst Person in the World, He Numbered the Pores on My Face* and the *Anxious* and *Ashamed* Bible studies. She writes regularly for *ParentLife* magazine, *HomeLife* magazine, and She Reads Truth. Scarlet enjoys speaking to women around the country about the freedom and rest available in Jesus. She and her husband live in Tennessee, where she loves sign language with her daughters, nachos by herself, writing for her friends, and studying stand-up comedy with a passion that should be reserved for more important pursuits.

Notes

1. Simon Turpin, "Did Moses Really Live 120 Years?" Answers in Genesis, March 20, 2023, https://answersingenesis.org/bible-questions/did-moses-really-live-120-years/#:~:text=Although%20Exodus%202:23%20simply,any%20evidence%20should%20be%20understood.

2. C. S. Lewis, *The Problem of Pain* (HarperCollins, 2001), 94–95.

3. C. H. Spurgeon, *Treasury of David, Psalm 1*, https://www.blueletterbible.org/Comm/spurgeon_charles/toc/ps001.cfm.

4. Blue Letter Bible, Strong's Lexicon H3045, s.v. *yāḏaḏ*, https://www.blueletterbible.org/lexicon/h3045/csb/wlc/0-1/.

5. William A. VanGemeren, *The Expositor's Bible Commentary,* Frank E. Gaebelein, ed. (Zondervan. 1991).

6. Timothy Keller quoting John Newton, Facebook, March 14, 2017, https://www.facebook.com/TimKellerNYC/posts/everything-is-necessary-that-god-sends-our-way-nothing-can-be-necessary-that-he-/1432364243470124/.

7. Some of this chapter originally appeared in an article I wrote in Peer Mag: https://peermag.org/articles/the-power-of-a-pillow-nest/.

8. David Mathis, "What Is the Hypostatic Union?" December 19, 2007, https://www.desiringgod.org/articles/what-is-the-hypostatic-union.

9. Michael J. Kruger, "Why Jesus's Humanity Matters as Much as His Divinity," *Gospel Coalition*, April 27, 2021, https://www.thegospelcoalition.org/article/jesus-humanity-matters-divinity/, emphasis original. See also Gregory of Nazianzus. (1994). Epistle 101: To Cledonius the Priest Against Apollinarius in Nicene and Post-Nicene Fathers, P. Schaff and H. Wace, eds., Vol. 7 (Hendrickson, 1994).

10. Eugene H. Peterson, *A Long Obedience in the Same Direction* (InterVarsity Press, 2019).

11. Tim Keller, Sermon: "Praying Our Tears," February 27, 2000, YouTube video, 20:24, https://youtu.be/DxOWWWVDGD0?si=T8bTwqMqxIl-noi_.

12. Keller, "Praying Our Tears," 21:54 referencing Derek Kidner's commentary Psalms 1–72 (or Psalms 73–150) (InterVarsity Press, 1973), 176.

13. Westminster Assembly, The Westminster Shorter Catechism (1647; Reprint Presbyterian Board of Christian Education), https://prts.edu/wp-content/uploads/2016/12/Shorter_Catechism.pdf.

14. C. S. Lewis, *Weight of Glory* (Zondervan, 2001), 26.

15. Eugene H. Merrill, Mark F. Rooker, and Michael A. Grisanti, *The World and the Word: An Introduction to the Old Testament* (B&H Academic, 2011), 398.

16. Jason DeRouchie, "Lecture on Ezekiel," MBTS Video Lecture, 13:19.

17. *The Gospel Project: From This World to the World to Come* (Lifeway Christian Resources, 2024), 126.

18. J. Scott Duvall, Revelation, ed. Mark L. Strauss and John H. Walton, Teach the Text Commentary Series (Baker Books, 2017), 314–15.

19. L. M. Montgomery, *Anne of Green Gables* (Penguin Classics, 2008), 38 (original work published 1908).

20. Timothy Keller, *Walking with God Through Pain and Suffering* (Penguin, 2013), 44.

21. Parts of this section originally appeared in a devotional Scarlet wrote for SheReadsTruth.com.

22. Stephanie Giang-Paunon, Fox News, August 16, 2024, https://www.foxnews.com/entertainment/snl-alum-victoria-jackson-battles-inoperable-cancer-death.

23. Dallas Gagnon, MassLive, August 16 2024, https://www.masslive.com/news/2024/08/former-saturday-night-live-star-reveals-terminal-cancer-battle.html#:~:text=Former%20%E2%80%9CSaturday%20Night%20Live%E2%80%9D%20actress,shared%20on%20her%20Instagram%2C%20Aug.

24. Leena Nasir, Daily Caller, August 16, 2024, https://dailycaller.com/2024/08/16/victoria-jackson-saturday-night-live-alum-cancer-mortality-health-medical-prescription-drugs/?utm_source=dlvr.it&utm_medium=facebook.

25. Eugene H. Peterson, *A Long Obedience in the Same Direction: Discipleship in an Instant Society* (InterVarsity Press, 2000).